Create Your Way To Freedom!

How To Be A Big Success From Someone Who Isn't!

by

Bob McGough

Contents

Foreword

As a full-time author, I can honestly say this is the hardest thing I've ever done. When I finished my first book, I thought I had achieved something—and I had, but then I discovered an entire side of the creative endeavor that I hadn't even thought about. The real work was about to begin. I knew I wanted to pursue writing as something more than just a hobby, but I didn't know where to start. I didn't know anyone in the author community, so I had no one to ask. So, I got into a small literary festival, and the people I met there started me on a path to success.

It took years of trial and error, but eventually I was able to leave the job I had spent twenty years of my life at climbing the corporate ladder. There are three things it takes to make a living as a creative: creativity (obviously), planning, and hustle. They're all important, but of the three, the hustle is the most important. It takes a lot to keep plugging away day in and day out without a guaranteed return. That's what impresses me about Bob. He can hustle with the best of 'em.

If you're like I was, this book is going to offer some valuable insights into what happens after you've typed "The End." What you'll find in these pages is experience it takes years to develop, giving you an invaluable head start toward your own creative freedom.

- Ben Meeks, Author of *The Art of Selling Books: A Sales Strategy For Authors*

Introduction

If you're reading this, then you're probably in the same place I was some years back. You probably have an image in your head of where you want to end up, but no real clear idea on how to get there. For me, it was locking in on the dream that I wanted to be a full-time writer. I knew what I wanted, but I had no concept of how to go from point A to point B, which led to a haphazard cycle of "try a thing -> watch that thing explode horribly -> try the next thing."

And that kinda sucks.

So, the fact that you're holding this book right now shows that you probably have more sense than I do! I myself never took the time to read any sort of guide or self-help book—well, except for *On Writing* by Stephen King, because that book is amazing. And part of what makes that book so awesome is that it's very autobiographical, which—besides being a lot more interesting than just the typical feel-good words you might find in self-help books—gives you real-world examples to show you how to be a better writer.

Now, I will begrudgingly admit that I am not Stephen King-level successful. Hell, I'm not even . . . well, pretty-much-any-author-you-can-think-of-level successful. You could even argue that by a lot of conventional standards, I'm not a big "success." But you know what? Fuck those conventional standards!

This book is going to show you how to tell "convention" to shove it and define success for yourself. It's going to teach you, using real-life examples drawn from my own lived experiences, how to use your creativity to get to where you want to be.

I've learned a lot over the past decade-plus of fumbling around, and I've been blessed to gather knowledge from a host of folks doing this whole "creative" thing a lot better than me. So, I am not saying I know exactly where the treasure is buried, but I dare say I at least have cobbled together most of a map, one with a few clues jotted down along the margins. And by following this book and learning from my pitfalls, maybe you will wander into far fewer "*here be dragons.*"

This book is loosely divided up into four sections. Once you get past this introduction and learn a bit about me, you'll find yourself in the "General Steps to Take" section. Here is where I lay out the broad steps you should be taking and offer some overall useful advice.

After you clear that hurdle, you'll be in the middle of "Finding Other Revenue Streams." Here is where I talk about how you can create a bunch of tiny streams of (often) passive income that will fund your war chest. It's something I'm somewhat well-known for amongst the circles I operate in.

Next, it's going to be all about transparency. Here, I'm going to get really autobiographical and show you how my career has played out to date, with as much relevant information as I can provide. We'll talk mental health, being an underachiever—all that fun stuff!

Lastly, I'll include a few simple guides that you can use to jumpstart the whole process. Simple enough, right?!

So, if you feel as though your life could use a change and you enjoy puns, light-to-moderate cursing, and self-deprecating humor, then come along for the ride. This is a book for the creative people of the world, dreaming dreams of all sizes. If that describes you at all, then you're in the right place!

Now, let's see what we can do to help make those dreams a reality.

Note: If you are too broke to afford this book, go to my website and contact me. I will send you a PDF copy for free. I've been helped out a lot along the way, and I'd be a real asshole if I hoarded this knowledge away from someone who really needed it just because they don't have a few spare bucks. Though, how will you read this if you don't already have the book? Quite the conundrum!

Who Am I? Why Should You Listen to Me?

I'm Bob, and I'm an author, podcaster, and indie TTRPG game designer from backwoods Alabama. I'm the Dictator for Life of the Tales by Bob Empire (what I call my business happenings), and I have been blessed to have a wonderfully bizarre and eventful life. Here are some highlights, in absolutely no particular order:

1. I've picked up dozens of hitchhikers over the years.

2. Sometimes elements of the fictional stories I write come true.

3. I once skinny-dipped (chunky-dunked?) at a wedding.

4. I run a small arts-focused nonprofit (besides the Tales by Bob Empire! *Oooo, sick burn*).

5. One time while searching for flint knapping material in a creek, a friend and I dug up a dead

cow thinking it might be a human cadaver.

6. Oh, I have a bachelors in anthropology. Which should help the above statement make fractionally more sense.

7. I've done press work for bands as diverse as Upchurch the Redneck to Stitches.

8. Yeah, I hadn't heard of them either.

9. I don't believe in the supernatural, but I used to go ghost hunting and give haunted tours.

10. I once wrote a book about fictional breeds of clams.

11. I was raised Mormon.

12. I've been the producer on a trio of music albums. No, you haven't heard of any of the bands.

13. I have my master's in music industry. Clearly, I don't love making money.

14. I had a stalker get a job where I worked and threaten to kill me a couple of times.

15. I'm an Eagle Scout.

16. Someone once hired me to write a *My Little Pony/Doctor Who* crossover erotica. I used it as

a chance to use as many horse-based puns as possible. They tipped me.

17. I broke my wrist in a wall of death at a Divine Heresy concert.

18. As of this moment, I have been to nine countries outside the US.

19. I have writing credits on a few small computer games and apps you've never played.

20. I still live in Alabama with my amazing LadyWife, Kiddo, and a clowder of increasingly portly cats.

"What does that have to do with the price of tea in China?" I can hear my dad asking from the grave. Nothing? Everything? I list those out to give you a little taste of what my life has been like, with the understanding that that's just the tip of the iceberg. My life has been unusually bizarre in a lot of ways, and spectacularly underwhelming in others.

I'm your typical conventional underachiever. Top 98th percentile on the MAT I took to get into grad school, full-ride scholarship for my undergrad, Duke TIP scholar, perfect 36 on the English portion of the ACT, etc.—then pair all that with a series of dead-end jobs for little pay in areas totally unrelated to either of my degrees. I got divorced and laid off within three months of each other when the economy tanked in

2008 and spent the next two years unemployed. I am the quintessential "*marches to the beat of his own drum*" kind of guy, with all the baggage that entails.

I'm just another broke-ass millennial from South Alabama, plugging away at life.

None of that is likely to inspire a lot of confidence—I get that. "Why on earth would I listen to a guy who lets possible serial killers into his car on the regular?" Fair.

I lay all that out to make a few points. First, I'm just a guy. I'm not Stephen King, I'm not Brandon Sanderson—I'm Bob. I'm no better than you; I just maybe have some knowledge that might be useful to you (much like you probably have for me). And while I would like to make a couple bucks from this book, I also genuinely want to help people out.

I like helping people, is my second point. From the hitchhikers I've given lifts to the artists I've helped through my nonprofit, I've tried to leave the world a better place than I found it, and I hope this can help you do the same. If you get some real value from this book, I hope you'll pass it on to someone else too. Let me know if you do, and I'll send you a PDF of it to keep, no charge.

Lastly, that list should show you that I'm going to be pretty real with you. If I'm putting things on there like "*dug up a dead cow because he's an idiot,*" then rest assured I am going to be straight with you on my actual real advice. I would imagine most of the advice books you've ever read have been written by people who were *actually* successful. Well, welcome to one written by someone who isn't! At least not in any easily recognizable way.

I'm going to give you realistic advice, advice from someone who, frankly, you are far more likely to end up like rather than Stephen King. So, when I tell you something, hopefully it rings a little more true than some millionaire in their mansion telling you how to wind up just like them.

Follow my path and you, too, can afford to live in Alabama—if you also have a day job!

It's not as catchy as "*How to make millions!*" but fuck me if it isn't more honest.

Section One: General Steps to Take

Here is where I lay it all out: the core pathway to creating your way to freedom. If you only read one section of this book, let it be this one!

Don't worry, I know it sounds boring, but I use a lot of weird examples from my own life to liven things up. It'll be fun! (For a self-help sort of book, at least.) So, let's dive in!

Mission Statement

First and foremost, all motivational pathways have to have a mission statement, right? And it absolutely *must* sound pretentious as all hell. It is a universal law, I believe, and who am I to try and buck the universe? I refuse to be *mission* out, so let's give it a go, shall we?

The *Create Your Way to Freedom* Mission Statement

Wait, screw that. We can do better on the title. Take two:

The *Create Your Way to Freedom* Manifesto of Awesomeness

Better! We'll call it a work in progress. Until we think of something better, let's jump right in:

Using our innate talents, we will help foster a culture in our lives that will lead us to a better, more successful, and more enriched place. Using our creativity will allow us to stand out and be noticed, helping us reach our goals.

Was that pretentious enough? Let's summarize it in real language now:

You have a skill.

Use it.

Get creative with your creativity.

Profit (maybe).

That is what this whole book is about. If you're a creative person, you already have the tools you need to break out of whatever rut you're in. I can't promise that you will, but I *can* attest that you have the attributes that have worked for millions of others to do so since the dawn of time. You just have to stop wasting time and start using what you have.

How to Do It

You want to know how to *Create Your Way to Freedom*?

Real talk? Put down this book, and whatever creative ability you have, go practice it. Then figure out how to use your creativity to get noticed so you can monetize your skills, or realize what other goal you might have. If you dig down deep, you probably already know what you should be doing, at least in a general sense.

And yet, here you are, still reading. Don't take direction very well, do you?

Well, I know I sure as hell don't, so maybe that's a pretty common trait amongst us creative types. Since you're still reading, I suppose I'll go into a bit more detail. Luckily this book is fairly short, so even if by some mistake you finish it, you won't have wasted too much time.

It's hard to make it out there these days. And for many creative people, the nine-to-five grind is a special form of hell, or it might not even be an option at all. Maybe you're a stay-at-home parent. Perhaps you're caught in a vicious cycle of debt. There are a huge number of reasons why conventional day/night jobs might not be what you need or want.

In my case, I've worked nights for the bulk of my adult life. I had the occasional offer come my way that would've gotten me off of nights and into the world of the living, but they were jobs that I knew with every fiber of my being would just suck the creativity right out of me. IT help desk? No thanks. I'll just keep fighting my circadian rhythm while sobbing into my daylight-bathed pillow, thank you very much.

Maybe you're just fine with the daily grind, but you're seeking just a little more out of life than coming home every day and turning on the TV till it's time to go to bed (zero judgment if that's what makes you happy!). Maybe, just maybe, you want a little recognition for your more unconventional abilities. Hell, it could be as simple as the need to just create something, *anything,* to scratch that creative itch, to get the ideas careening around your mind down onto paper.

Whatever your reason for seeking a life different from the one you have now, creativity is going to be your key. The world is only getting more and more populous, and unless your particular brand of creativity is building and using weapons of mass destruction like space lasers, that's probably not going to change anytime soon. So, it's becoming ever more important to either stand out from the crowd or, more likely, be better at directing the crowd to you in new ways.

Let's take a moment for an example:

There are a ton of people out there writing fiction today. Fantasy, steampunk, horror—those genres have writers in the hundreds of thousands. And with self-publishing becoming ever easier, the market is only becoming ever more glutted, to the point of ridiculousness in many cases. And now we have AI on the scene? Fuck me.

So, imagine you're an author out there, writing away on your first fantasy novel. You are a smart, creative person, and you feel sure you have something of quality to get out there for the world to embrace. This could be all you need to escape from that warehouse job you wish you could be free from.

You write it up, slave over it, and release it into the aether of the internet. Now, any number of things could happen, but for most people it will likely be one of these:

1. It turns out that you are the next coming of George R. R. Martin, only you finish books in a timely fashion. That perfect trendsetter stumbles onto your book by chance. Word of mouth quickly spreads across BookTok, and the people flock to you in droves. Jealousy consumes me, and I implode into a black hole of envy.

2. You are a perfectly competent writer, maybe even a great one, but no one sees your books among the tsunami of books that hit Amazon each and every day. You're someone who just

needs a little help to draw eyes to your books, and this is where word of mouth comes in. So, you start to use your creativity to get noticed. Maybe you decide to write a self-help book to help draw more eyes to them. Maybe you call it *Create Your Way to Freedom*—who knows.

3. Turns out, you suck at writing. No one buys your stuff. You start to drink heavily, which you think makes you even more of a writer. Maybe it helps. Most likely it doesn't. In this case, I recommend you either keep honing your skills before you try again or find a new creative outlet. You're creative; you'll come up with something. Or maybe you won't. Stop looking at me like that!

The point I'm trying to make, in a way too long and wordy fashion, is that it's more likely that while you *are* creative, you're not super exceptional. **DO NOT FEEL BAD.** If everyone were exceptional, then no one would be exceptional—that's the whole point of the damn word. As your fellow non-exceptional person, at least you're in decent company!

So, we've established that you're probably not exceptional. Don't worry, I won't tell your mother; she wouldn't believe me anyway. And if by some chance you are exceptional, I'm sorry. Please remember me fondly when you're rich. Maybe buy a few dozen copies of this book to send to all your friends with this passage highlighted, having paid some lowly freelancer to scrawl "Lol, this ain't me" in the margins of each copy.

Anyway, if you're not exceptional, that's perfectly fine. You're creative! That's better than being *only* exceptional. Of course, it would be better to be both, but damn it, you've got to work with what you got. As a creative person with good ideas, you're in great company. The only problem is that there is a lot of that company . . . and it sometimes smells funny.

So here is what's going to separate you from the masses who are steadily plodding along, churning out page after page, drawing after drawing, song after song of perfectly good creative work: **creative ways of getting your ideas out there**.

Once you reach a certain amount of popularity, then the whole "spreading the word" thing will start to somewhat handle itself (never fully, though). But initially, you HAVE to find a way to stand out, to get your stuff in front of the eyes of people in such a way that they will actually notice you.

What is that way? Well, if I knew for certain, this book wouldn't be as cheap as it is. Part of the problem is that by its very nature, that *thing* that makes you stand out needs to be different for everyone, at least to a degree. For me, I sometimes dress up as my main character (in a mullet wig, jorts, and a Hawaiian shirt) and stand on street corners holding a sign that says "Read Redneck Wizard Books." Sometimes it works.

Sometimes it doesn't. One time, it got a gun brandished at me.

But for those times that it doesn't work, I started a podcast. Then a second. Then made a line of shirts. And then wrote a bizarre book on fictional clams. The point is, I'm putting myself out there in a way I haven't really seen a lot of other people try. And hopefully, if nothing else, I will have helped a few people along the way—and given fictional clams the press they so richly deserve.

So, take some time to think of what might work for you. You **are** creative, damn it; you can do this. Think of ways to catch people's eye. And in the meantime . . .

Use It or Lose It

In the end, there's really one thing that really sets you apart from the vast majority of folks out there: actually using your creativity. If I had a dollar for every person I knew who wasted their talents by simply not using them, I would be able to hire a lot more editors! There are so many good artists out there who just never use their skill. As a guy with all the artistic ability of an inebriated snail, it drives me wild! One of best writers I know (far better than me), you can't really call him a writer, because he doesn't write.

It frustrates me to see this happen. There are a million reasons why it does, too many to even try to really go into. Suffice it to say, though, for every person who gets out there and does something, *anything,* there are a dozen people who instead spend the commercial breaks of that hip new show complaining about how their life sucks and doesn't fulfill them. They sit there and watch life pass them by, and then wonder how it happened.

You can be different from that. Damn it, you have the potential! All it takes is for you to just take the plunge and actually use your abilities. You may fail, but at least when you're on your deathbed, you'll know you tried. I haven't been on my deathbed yet (though a few hangovers have come pretty close), but I like to think that will be some solace.

I tell everyone the reason I can write as much as I do is because of NaNoWriMo (National Novel Writing Month). Over the course of November you write fifty thousand words, which is a ton of words in a pretty short length of time, no two ways about it. That said, my first year trying, I completed it. It was a beast, but I did it. At that point I had only written perhaps two short stories, and then in just a month I cranked out thousands upon thousands of words.

It showed me what I could do when challenged. When you can write an average of 1,600 words a **day** for a month, what's cranking out 5,000 over the course of a month? If you wrote just 200 words a day, Monday through Friday, for a year, that would be 52,000 words. That's enough for a shorter novel. Now, what if you did that and then paired it with NaNoWriMo? Then you'd have around 100,000 words, which is a fantastic length for most any sort of novel you could want to craft. As a point of reference, this paragraph by itself is about 120 words. Can you find the time to write two paragraphs a day? I bet you can.

Creativity is a muscle; you need to use it and test it to reach your full potential. If you want my advice—which, as you are this far along, I assume you do—give the following a try:

Find a similar test, be it NaNoWriMo, some thirty-day art challenge, finally hitting the studio, or whatever is relevant to your brand of creativity. Push yourself as hard as you can for a few weeks to a month—really throw yourself out there. Obviously, what with working a day job/raising kids/etc., this sort of pace would be unsustainable over the long term. But if you're really serious about this, surely you can keep up the pace for a month, right?

Then, when it comes time to do the more reasonable daily grind, it will seem so much easier to you, and you'll be secure in the knowledge of what you can accomplish when pressed. What's writing 200 words a day when you've done 1,600 for thirty days in a row?

A piece of advice I hold to with my work is this: Treat it like a part-time job. Because that's what it is, damn it, until one day—when you work hard and have a bit of luck—it becomes your full-time job. So, set aside enough hours each week to practice or produce, and keep doing it week in and week out. Soon enough, it will become a habit!

Train Your Brain

"But Bob," come the plaintive wails, "I want to write that book/paint that picture/write that song, but whenever I actually make the time, nothing comes out. What do I do?" Which is a good question, and one with no one-size-fits-all answer. But I will tell you what has generally helped me out.

You see, humans are super easy to train. I mean, our brains are super strange and powerful, full of mystery and wonderment, but they're also easier to train than dogs half the time. You just have to get out of your own way. So, here is my quick and easy hack to train yourself to be creative.

Step one is to figure out a good spot to be creative. For me, that's my home office desk, but for you it may be the couch, the kitchen table, or your bed. The exact spot isn't what's important here; it's that you always go to the *same* spot. So, pick a place that's comfy and where you can easily do whatever work it is you want to do with few distractions.

Next, pick some music that won't be a distraction. For me, I have a go-to band and album—*Sunset Mission* by Bohren and Der Club of Gore. It's wordless German funeral doom jazz. I can listen to it endlessly on loop without ever worrying that it will distract me. It's calm, low, and has no words. Perfect.

The next step—which I don't always do because I am a walking fire hazard with this beard—is to light a candle with a scent, one that you really like and won't get sick of. Or maybe it's incense, or one of those wall plug-in thingies my LadyWife is always setting up. Just make sure it's the same scent every time.

Now, each time you want to be creative, all you have to do is go to your special place, play your creative music, and light that same scented candle. Do this EVERY time. Will the words flow at first? Probably not, but once you've done this enough times, they will. Your brain will then be properly trained that this place + this scent + this sound = creative time.

Easy.

It's All About Who You Know

Not really—I just needed an eye-catching headline in case the last few sections were too preachy and I was losing you. In truth, it's only partly about who you know.

What that means is, no one succeeds in complete isolation. The more people you have on your side, the easier it will become to reach your goal. Word will spread about your endeavors a lot faster if you have all your friends sharing your work on Facebook, Pinterest, etc. instead of you just yelling at people passing by from your porch . . . though I guess that could depend on the quality of your yelling, and how slow a news day it is.

Seriously, though, it's the other creatives that you meet and network with who will likely be the largest help! It's one thing for your great-aunt Doris to share a picture you took to her friends on Facebook. It's on a whole other level entirely to have built a connection with a famous photographer at a convention who then shares your work to their following.

Let me give you some examples:

During Covid, I started publishing my redneck wizard books. Despite the fact that *The Dresden Files* is by far the most popular urban fantasy series out there, male-fronted urban fantasy isn't a big-selling genre right now. Most of the really popular UF is female-fronted, and definitely doesn't feature protagonists with a crippling meth addiction.

Go figure.

Anyway, I started putting these books out while essentially locked away in my home. There were no conventions happening, so I was really just spreading the word via social media at that point. It went . . . ok.

But then, once the world began to reopen a bit, I was able to go to Dragon Con once more. I went to a panel, and wouldn't you know it, there was a guy on said panel who was also writing male-fronted urban fantasy set in the Deep South!

And that is how I met Ben Meeks. We chatted, shook hands, exchanged email addresses, and then over the next few weeks we started swapping emails back and forth. Here are a few tangible things that have come out of that relationship:

1. I have been invited to sell books with him at a bunch of conventions all over. By splitting booth fees and hotel costs, we've both saved hundreds of dollars, changing break-even weekends into profitable ones.

2. Through him, I came to meet Nancy (an

absolute legend in the southeastern literary scene) and Venessa (who runs The Writers' Troupe), connections that have gotten me on all sorts of panels at conventions. It's because of them that I have gotten to be on a panel with the likes of Sherrilyn Kenyon. (She's sold seventy million copies of her books. She probably sold more copies of her books during the time it took you to read this chapter than I have sold of mine all week.)

3. He connected me with the fine folks at the Atlanta Self-Publishing Conference, which led to my first paid professional presenter gig, which is where I connected with Stuart Jaffe (who is much better at all this than me. Does he have a book? I should go look . . .).

And those things are all great, don't get me wrong. Money? Opportunities to stoke my ego? I'll take those all day! But what has likely benefited me the most has been the *intangibles*. Here's a list:

1. He taught me how to sell in person. I mean, obviously I had sold stuff in person before, but I wasn't good at it. He taught me so many little tips and tricks that have really upped my game. He actually wrote a book about it, and you should go get it. (*The Art of Selling Books: A Sales Strategy for Authors* by Ben Meeks—it's on Amazon.)

2. It's been so good for my mental health to have someone else in the same trenches as me, someone to share ideas and complaints with. Having someone with the same struggles as you to help share the mental load? That's priceless. Writing is lonely work.

So, be a nice person, get out there, and make some connections. It will pay off in the long run! I would promise you that, but you might not be all that nice, and then you're going to blame me when it doesn't happen, and I just don't need that in my life right now.

Let's do another example about me, because I enjoy writing those:

A guy I went to grad school with started a comic convention. We weren't close, but we knew each other well enough that six years out of grad school we could go, "Oh, hey, it's you." So, I reached out and offered to host a panel on the state of the publishing industry and how to get published (and I will do the same for you, at your con, if you let me!).

After the panel wrapped up (I spoke to an impressive crowd of maybe four people), one of the attendees came up to me at my booth to follow up on some questions. As it turned out, he co-owned a brewery, and when he realized I also did a booze-themed literary podcast, he invited the podcast (me) on the spot to come be in his brewery's harvest festival. Since then, I have been in three different events at this very cool emporium of ginger beer—all because I was nice and helpful, and not a dick to a guy who just wanted a little bit of my time.

Years later, he invited me to a book club that meets at his house, and I sold about a hundred bucks worth of books and got a free meal out of it. I will happily talk to your book club, too, especially if you feed me. Just saying.

Do we have time for one more example? Well, as I am penning this, yes—yes I do. Here goes:

I have always made an effort to support my fellow side-hustlers. From as little as sharing their Facebook pages to taking time out to help mentor them, I have made an effort to put out the kind of support I like to receive (to mixed results). This paid off one day when a young side-hustler I'd been mentoring pointed out an author event a few towns over I hadn't heard of.

So I applied, and I got in. Day of, I showed up on time, had all my ducks in a row, and made a point to be helpful to the hosts as well as my fellow attendees. Karma instantly paid off when I got stuck in what I came to think of as the "cool corner"—the booths to either side of me were a bit edgier than the usual South Alabama author event mix of Christian/"My Memaw's Tales" types of releases. They were my sort of people.

When the event was over, the librarian in charge who I'd hit it off with ended up inviting me to come back and help host two panels when their local nerdy convention rolled around! It was perfect! I got to host two panels (to a crowd approaching ten in number this time—hey, it's progress), and add them to my steadily growing resume of public speaking engagements. Which, outside of penning over-the-top self-help books, is my favorite way of trying to spread the gospel of the Tales by Bob Empire these days.

Show up early, have your shit together, and be nice. It will pay dividends, I can virtually assure you.

Going off the networking theme, I can already hear some of you fine folks out there reading this. "But Bob, I'm an introvert! There's no way I can talk to people like that!"

That's fine. You don't have to. I'm not your parental figure, calm down.

Couple points, though: First, you will have a harder time of it without these connections. It sucks, but you will. Without networking, you're going to miss out on a ton of opportunities. You won't hear about potential upcoming events, you won't hear the backroom author gossip about what publishers to avoid, you won't learn hard-won tips and tricks. None of these things are deal-breakers, but they will help your path immensely.

Next, I'm an introvert myself. But you know what? That doesn't mean I can't talk to folks! That just means that when the convention is over, I'm going to spend a couple days holed up in my office *not* talking to folks while I recharge my social battery.

I am, however, usually pretty bad at small talk, which has little to do with introversion and everything to do with me being a weird little shit. Lovable, but weird. And you know what? I just kept at it, and eventually I got better. Just like I didn't come out of the womb penning the world's finest meth wizard fantasy novels, I didn't come out equipped with a glib networky tongue. But in both cases, I practiced. Because it was, and is, important.

Practice it—it will pay off. Or don't, but then don't complain that it's coming a little slower than you would like. Or if you do complain, don't do it to me at least! Unless you have snacks. Then feel free to share your snacks and complain away. Chips are a good start. Sour cream and cheddar are the best.

"But I Have No Skill!"

Another complaint I have heard over and over is: "Bob, I am creative, but I don't have a skill. I have all these great ideas but no way to get them out there."

Assuming you aren't just lazy, you can *learn* a skill. For example, I got tired of having to pay folks for graphic design work; it was really cutting into my publishing war chest. So you know what? I bought the Affinity suite of products (get fucked, Adobe), watched some YouTube videos, and started practicing. Now, I make all my own promo images, shirt designs, and most of my book covers (if they aren't *too* complicated). The cover on this book? I made it. Saved myself a couple hundred bucks in doing so.

You can do the same, provided you have the time and inclination. That doesn't mean you'll be the next Leonardo da Vinci, Peter Steele, or Edgar Allen Poe, of course, but you will be able to create and get those ideas out of your head and into the world.

But maybe you don't have the time, or you have some sort of disability that prevents you from learning a skill. Totally understandable! Here is where network-ing will once more come into play.

If the idea is good enough, and you work at it, you can surely find some people who share your vision. Have an idea for a comic book? Flesh that idea out as much as humanly possible, and then start talking to artists. Actually write up a legitimate, properly format-ted script. If your idea has merit, they will see it.

Quick aside: I'm an author, and I love talking to other authors, whether they've just started out or have been doing this for decades. You know what I hate, though? Someone walking up to tell me their book idea in hopes I will write it for them. I promise you, what-ever author you're talking to already has more books in mind than they have time to write. They do not want to write your idea. Authors would almost always love to help give you advice on writing it for yourself, but don't waste your time and ours talking about books neither of us—let's be real—are ever gonna write. But if you had an actual fleshed-out outline in your hands that showed you had done more than just think about the plot in the shower, I would be fractionally more inclined to listen to you positively.

Anyhoo, engage with people whenever you get a chance. I have a steadfast rule to try to respond to any comments made on any of my social media pages. If someone is taking the time out of their day to look at what I'm doing, and then comments on it, the very least I can do is respond in kind. It's led to me leaving some pretty inane comments back, but by god, they are getting engagement!

Let's dive back in to another example from the life of Bob:

I used to follow a seemingly delightful person on one of my social media accounts that I thought was doing a great job of being inspirational. They posted regularly and always appeared to try to engage their audience, seeking input from their followers with every post. Sadly, I almost never saw any sort of response from them, and as a guy who would love more engagement on my own posts, I resolved to start answering any question they posed that I could in any way relate to. I wanted people to do the same on my posts, so I resolved to be the change I wanted to see.

It was admittedly a little harder than I anticipated, because just then, the person made a spate of posts about things I could not relate to. But I bided my time, and soon enough they wound up back in my wheel-house. So, boom! Response. Boom! Another response. For a weeks' worth of posts, I hit them with as good a message as I could muster.

And I got one halfhearted reply. *One*, in response to about a week of comments. So, I stopped. Because eventually you will come to realize that some people don't want conversation; they want an audience. Which is perfectly fine—just don't expect folks to come through for you when you really need it.

Everyone wants to feel special. If you can make them feel that way, they will be far more inclined to support you. Listen to their views on a subject, and they'll be more willing to share the link to your latest YouTube video. Scratch their back, and they will scratch yours.

It's fairly shitty to expect other people to support what you have going on if you, in turn, do not support others. People notice things like that, and you would be surprised to what degree! As a big believer in karma, I firmly hold that being a douche like that will come back to haunt you. We should all be helping each other, at all times.

One of the men I consider a mentor is John G. Hartness. He often talks about how no matter how quickly he writes, there's no way he can write as fast as people read. He can't possibly write all the books a person could ever want to read, so therefore it doesn't hurt him in the least to share other folks' work. "A rising tide lifts all boats," as he is wont to say. He's an author and a publisher with scads of his own books, plus all of his many authors' books. And yet he still shares my books whenever I put one out, even though he had nothing to do with them (other than, you know, being my hero).

Each of us is struggling every day to reach our goals, and if you can spare just a little bit of love and energy for others, it will pay off in the long run. I know a woman a bit farther along in this whole process than I, and I have always made a point of helping her out any way that I can. So, now that success is starting to come her way, she hires me out when she can to write for her.

Now, I am not saying you should help people for the money; help people because it's the right thing to do. Because in all of this, in my mind, there is an element of . . .

Morality

Now, keeping in mind that I wrote a self-help book to not-so-subtly try to get people to buy my other books, I am maybe *not* the moral authority of the new century. That said, I do try to live life as a pretty decent chap, though, so maybe give me a tiny touch of credence.

In all of this, I firmly believe you have a moral obligation to help others along this path. Jokes aside, it's actually a large part of the reason I wrote this book. I believe that as someone trying hard to make my life a little bit better and relying on my fellow man to help make it happen, I have a responsibility to be as inspiring, positive, and helpful as I can.

If you start achieving your goals and then start belittling those who haven't had your success, then you are the lowest sort of asshole. Build people up, don't tear them down. I assure you, people will take note. I can't count the number of authors whose names carry far more weight than my own who have nevertheless been so warm and genuine to me. And I also remember, with the cold hatred of a million imploding suns, those who have acted as though they're way too big-time to consort with a peasant like me. (Ok, it was only one guy, and he wasn't even an author. But fuck you, nameless guy who I still remember many hate-filled years later.)

Think of ways you can pay back the help you receive from others. For example, if I have the time, I'll help people write business plans or work on their resume, for free. I've gotten a ton of help just to get as far as I have, and it's the very least I can do. For me, it's a small thing since writing comes fairly easy to me, but to someone who just needs a resume to get that better job, it can mean the world.

Be the change you want to see in the world.

Claim Your Turf!

This next snippet of advice is less about how to build your pathway forward, but more on how to protect it. It's also the site of Bob's biggest regret as a creative. Stay tuned!

Social media is great—and essential—for anyone doing any sort of creative side hustle these days. No matter how much you hate it, you need to get on it. I don't care how good you are at whatever it is you do; if folks can't see it, they won't care. And folks' eyes are on social media.

I'll be honest: I **haaaate** social media. Despite that, I'm still on there. In fact, at this point in my career, I spend more time doing marketing, back-end stuff, and networking than I do writing most days. And the bulk of that takes place on social media.

That said, places like Facebook, Twitter, Instagram, and Tumblr are always changing their rules in ways that you have absolutely no control over. Take Tumblr, for example. They had a problem with folks using their platform to share child porn, so they decided to change the rules so that absolutely nothing even remotely resembling nudity, pornography, naked art, etc. could be shared on their site.

Folks didn't react all that well, as a lot of people viewed it as an overreaction or a way of punishing folks who had nothing to do with the problem. Me, I was nonplussed; my Tumblr account got far and away the least interaction of any of my social media accounts. (Tumblr isn't the best site for writer self-promotion, to say the least.) But those pissed-off folks left in droves. Site traffic tanked to a large degree. So, I just closed my Tumblr account and never looked back, having a good reason to now that everyone was gone.

But if you were one of the artists who used Tumblr as your site to take commission orders, well, you were patently screwed. Countless artists and the like went out of business because of this change or had to hurriedly move to another platform and try and rebuild their model on the fly. Needless to say, that was less than ideal.

So, your goal should always be to get people to your own turf. In most cases, that's going to be a website. Get your own website, because there—within reason—*you* set the rules. You may wake up one day and decide to do something dumb on your site, sure, but at least you'll have the power to undo it if that happens.

If you take commissions, yes, use all the available social media to get people's attention. But once you have that attention, direct them to your own website! Get your fans in the habit of going to your website so that if Facebook decides to suddenly throttle page views in favor of groups (which they have, as of writing this), you won't be quite as screwed as other people.

The internet changes so rapidly that you need to always be prepared for your primary means of reaching your potential customers to unexpectedly go away or change dramatically. You never know when an egotistical billionaire is going to buy the social media platform you're on and invite back all the Nazis. If you aren't ready, and if you need to be one of the millions who decided to dip out of that whirlwind, you are going to be in a real bind.

But you know what? Websites cost money, and maybe you don't have a lot of that to spare—I know I usually don't. The good news is, there's a bit of turf that doesn't cost you anything: Linktree! Or other sites like it! At the end of the day, a website is really just a link aggregator for you. That's what a Linktree is, and they're free. And one day, when you have more money and have a website of your own, you can put a link to it on your Linktree.

But website or Linktree aside, there is another form of turf that reigns supreme, at least from a marketing perspective:

Email lists!

Also known as "that thing that Bob regrets not having started a decade earlier," email lists using sites like Mailerlite don't cost you anything (at least until you have more subscribers than I currently have). Study after study has shown that this is your single best marketing tool, and also usually the cheapest.

If you have a website, it *needs* to have an email list sign-up page or link. If you have a Linktree, you need to have that connected to your sign-up page as well. If you're selling or presenting in person, you need to have either a sign-up sheet available or a QR code that connects to your Linktree (which in turn connects to your sign-up page). Seriously, *always* be trying to gather email addresses from interested parties.

As a quick aside, I can attest from personal experience that having a physical sign-up sheet of some sort typically works better than a QR code. Are QR codes better? I'd say yes, by pretty much any objective standard. But do people seem to just not use them? Also yes. This was one of the precious few things I was able to teach Ben Meeks when it came to in-person sales. He witnessed me get probably four times the number of sign-ups on my sheet than he got with his QR code.

Now, he uses both.

I would think this goes without saying, but just in case: Don't be annoying with your emails. If you generate a ton of great content, then a weekly email may work out for you. I know some bigger-name authors who do this, and they can get away with it because they generally are doing this full-time and can take the time to whip up an amazing email each week. Brian Keene is a great example.

Odds are, at this point, you either don't have that sort of time or that sort of content generation. The vast bulk of authors I know do an email once a month. That seems to be the sweet spot for keeping your name on people's minds without being annoying.

In summary: when it comes to social media, shit happens, but if you've been doing a good job training your people to open your emails and go to your own website, then you'll be alright.

Online Marketing

As I've already stated, marketing sucks. It's never fun, the rules are always changing, and oftentimes you're expected to spend money to really get ahead in the game. So far, I have mostly refused to spend said money, so yeah, I am not really "ahead." But I do a better job than some people out there, so here we go with my evergreen rules for online marketing.

The most important tip I can give is to be selective in your social media usage. This is twofold advice.

First, it's better to not have a presence on a social media platform at all than to have a page you're not using. If people go to your Facebook page and don't see any sort of recent post, they're going to assume that you don't do this anymore. As a result, they will take their limited time and very limited money and go give it to someone else.

I wasn't keen on Tumblr and posted only rarely, so I shut that page down. When Twitter got bought, I held my nose for a bit and kept posting, but that lasted about a week or so before I just totally stopped. For a while, I kept up a pinned post saying, "Hey, find me at all these other better places!" Then when the train went totally off the rails, I just shut it down. I knew I was no longer comfortable posting there, so there was no reason for me to be on there anymore.

This also goes for your blog. This is a hard one for folks (that's what she said)—it is so much easier to post a picture on Instagram or a link on Facebook. Blog posts take work, even if they are half-assed. But lord, I have been to *so many* authors' websites where their most recent blog post is from YEARS ago. You're a writer—you can't find the time to write *one* blog post every few months? Really? Trust me when I say it makes your site look so dead!

The other thing to be mindful of is sticking to the sites you understand or can come to understand. For example, I have a decent amount of luck promoting my work on Reddit. But the thing about Reddit is that if you don't do it in *just* the right way, they are going to roast you into oblivion. The place is a cesspool—one that I love, mind you, but a cesspool nonetheless. They will savage you if you don't understand the right way to go about things.

The inverse of that was Tumblr—I just didn't get it. I mean, I could make a post, sure. But commenting? Understanding comment chains? I probably could've figured it out, but I didn't really like how the site operated, so I never felt that compelled to learn how to work it properly. When it came to Twitter, I understood it, but I never really felt all that comfortable with it. I felt like I was always a half step away from putting my foot in my mouth, and thus I didn't use it as deftly as I used other sites.

You also have to consider what type of content you're creating. As an author, it can be hard to generate Instagram content, but it's a fantastic site for artists. And if you're a musician, then you need to be on Bandcamp. But also consider who your target market is and what social media sites they prefer. Instagram skews younger, Facebook skews older. Twitter is more combative, Tumblr is more supportive. If you're writing a cozy mystery about an elderly man with depression, then you might have more luck on Facebook/Tumblr than Instagram/Twitter (though every site will have its nooks and niches if you can find them). So, figure out what socials you like/are good at, and ignore the rest.

Some folks will advise you to go at least snag your username on other social media sites. That's good advice, I suppose, though I have only rarely followed it. You only have so much bandwidth, so many hours in the week, so pick your battlegrounds. If you get big enough to the point that you have to seriously worry about folks impersonating you, you can probably afford to pay someone to run your social media accounts and go claim all those usernames for you. That's the dream, at least.

Once you've selected where you're going to virtually hang out, then you need to follow this one fundamental piece of advice: bring value to whatever space you are in.

If all you ever do is post ads for your books, you're never going to get great fans who are looking to engage with you. Folks will pretty quickly start to tune you out, if they ever pay you much attention in the first place. But if you bring value to the space—be it by making memes, generating discussion about a related fandom, reviewing other books, doing fun little cover song videos, etc.—then folks will want to engage with you.

It's example time!

So, as an author who's been doing this for a good number of years, I've learned a lot. As such, there are a few topics I feel that I do better at than a decent number of people, like organic marketing and diversifying your revenue streams. I'm not the next coming of Steve Jobs, but I know what I'm about. I have things I can say that folks will learn from.

That has led to me saying those things in workshops, blog posts, and YouTube videos. I'm basically building up a whole little curriculum (a lot of which is included in this book, obviously), and so I have also started hosting all this content on my website. Several of the guides in the back section of this book are hosted there almost word for word. If I teach a workshop, I usually then take the PowerPoint I used to teach it and turn it into a YouTube video.

I share all this content for free. And whenever I stumble upon someone seeking a bit of knowledge that I have written about or made a video for, I can post a link back to my site. That way, I'm providing value to them (hopefully) as well as anyone who finds their way to that question in the future. And you know what? They've now visited my site to partake in that knowledge!

My hope is that over time, folks will be "trained" to go to my site to find all sorts of useful guides, and eventually they'll start going around to the other pages on my site to see what I do. This will lead to more book sales, more podcast listens, more shirts sold, more games bought—you get the idea.

That's what I'm banking on happening, at least.

Another example that has stuck with me is Gail Z. Martin. She is a huge *Supernatural* fan. *Huge.* Like, "runs groups for it" huge. And while she's in these spaces, talking with other fans and engaging in all the usual elements of fandom, she doesn't flog people over the head with links to her books.

But you know what? Over time, folks come to realize she's an author and they "follow her home." *Supernatural* fans and people who love the types of books she writes are less a Venn diagram and more a big circle, so it's a natural fit. She gets to enjoy talking about her passion, and in a roundabout way, she gets fans.

My last little example, which I'll discuss more in-depth in another section, is my push for transparency. I am constantly doing blog posts where I peel back the curtain and show people just how much I make, how many books I sell, etc. These are very inside-base-ball-type posts that will really only appeal to other authors, but people take value from them. I put that out there because I wish other authors would too. The more information shared, the better. And I'm pretty sure that I've gotten sales through these posts, though I don't do it for that reason.

So yeah: be intentional with your choice of social media, then provide value.

And if you've got it, spend a shitload of money on ads, I guess.

In-Person Marketing

One day, back when we had just started dating, I was having dinner with the LadyWife's family. It was the first time I had spent a significant amount of time with her parents and, being parents, they asked what I do for a living. "I'm a clerk at a warehouse!" I responded, wrapping my lips around some cornbread. "And I'm trying to be a writer."

You could have sliced thick cheese with the look my now LadyWife cut me. Her head twisted toward me so fast, I think I saw a biscuit get caught in the updraft. "No!" she declared. "He's not **TRYING** to be a writer. He **IS** a writer. He's been published, and you can find his stuff on Amazon."

We all went back to our respective noshes (I was plowing through a country fried steak with much aplomb), but that moment has stuck with me. Because she was 100% correct—I *am* an author. I was just a bit bashful about it. Whenever someone would ask, I always responded the same way: I'm TRYING, not I AM.

And I have worked to get better about that! I'm not Stephen King, but I'm certainly no slouch! I like to think I've been doing a much better job about selling myself since then. Because if I don't, who will? (Well, obviously the LadyWife, but she's a bit biased. Brilliant, but biased.)

So, step one is to be better about singing your own praises. Seriously, you rock, and you need to embrace that fact! I know I get really self-deprecating throughout this book, but that's just my style of humor. When I'm at events talking to the masses, I am much more confident-sounding about what I do. I'll still crack jokes, of course, but they tend to be more in the vein of "Can you believe someone let me out of Alabama?"

If you aren't doing this currently, it's just going to take some practice. And let it be known that there is a fine line between being confident in your craft and being an egotistical jackass. Trust me, folks will look at you far more favorably for sounding confident and asking a good question rather than acting as if you know everything.

Where exactly is that line? Good question! It's different for everyone, and if you notice that folks are avoiding you like the plague, then you've probably crossed over the line. That's about all I can tell you.

Let me give you an example of what *not* to do. I was at a convention, hanging out at my table in the author's alley, trying to sling some books. There was one author there who was new to doing events, as they had only just put out their first book. Rather loudly, they would expound at length to anyone who entered their orbit about how that person should be doing things.

When a guy who just put out his first book is telling John G. Hartness, in way too many words, just how he needs to be conducting his business . . . well, understandably, things went horribly awry. Every other author in the alley was taking note, and if you think we aren't Gossipy Guses when there aren't customers around, well, then you don't know authors very well. And we all have surprisingly long memories for that type of thing, so don't be that guy.

My other tip for marketing yourself in-person is to get into unexpected spaces. Obviously you want to be in libraries, conventions, and bookstores if you're an author. That's a given. But . . .

Oooo, let's do another example from the life of Bob!

Sticking with the author example, think about what your books are about. My series is about a redneck wizard. So, I threw on a mullet wig, a pair of jorts, a Hawaiian shirt, and made a big-ass sign that said "Read Redneck Wizard Books." Now that I was dressed as my main character, I went to where there was a hunting supply convention going on in the next town.

This event draws thousands of folks who like to go hunting so much that they'll travel to see a bunch of . . . hell, I don't know what they actually have inside the convention. Deer stands? Targets? Camouflage displays that you can't see? I didn't actually go inside;

I just stood on a street corner outside with a stuffed possum sitting on top of a stack of my books.

I got some looks, that's for sure.

But you know what? I was damn sure the only person promoting their books on the street corner that day! I caught people's attention, and I had a number of folks take a picture of me or scan my QR code that I had taped to the back of the sign. It might not have been the most book-focused crowd, but anyone in that crowd who liked to read was sure to take a closer look. These were people I likely would never have encountered in any of the conventional ways people market books. And, at a later event, I had someone tell me that they saw me that day as they drove by, looked me up, and were really enjoying book one. So, there's that!

I also witnessed a trio of rednecks and a homeless guy threaten to shoot each other, but that was unrelated to me. My life is never dull, though, I gotta say. Alabama, never change. Or please do, actually.

And that is what it may take for you. Remember how I talked about how being creative was going to be your edge? Things like this get you noticed. My goal is to do this enough times that I get on the news. That would be huge for me! And since you're reading this, I bet it would be huge for you too!

I will also point out an added benefit that I gained from my "dress like Howard Marsh and stand on street corners" ad campaign: It's helped make me quick on my feet when it comes to talking to people. In a convention space, you tend to wind up having the same sorts of interaction over and over. Every so often, though, you get thrown a curveball by a passerby, be it an odd question, a distinctive style, or what have you.

But being out on the street with a huge variety of passersby all moving quickly from point A to point B, you get a *lot* of practice coming up with quick interactions. You have a very limited window in which to talk to someone and potentially hook them into stopping to talk! And unlike at a convention where you can compliment their cosplay, you don't always have an easy "handle" on random people you come across. So, this *unconventional* tactic has really helped hone my in-person speaking skills.

In-Person Sales

Marketing is one thing, but actually selling? That's a different sort of animal. Let's dive in to what has worked for me, as an author. I don't have firsthand experience here, but I would imagine that as an artist or musician, the audio/visual component makes all this advice somewhat moot. So, take it for what it's worth.

Step one is, you really need to nail your pitch. Imagine someone walks up to your booth at a convention and you only have about five seconds to hook them. If you take too long, their eyes will glaze over—I've seen it soooo many times—and if you don't give them enough, they won't have anything to latch on to.

Want to know my pitch?

"I write a series about a redneck wizard with a crippling meth addiction solving backwoods occult mysteries."

I've said it so many times now that it just flows naturally. And yes, a lot of time I get a wide-eyed, somewhat scared look as they slowly back away. But you know what? *Those people wouldn't have liked my book anyway.* And for every slow walk away, I get a "Oh my god, what?! Ok, you have my attention!" or some variation thereof.

Hook 'em, and hook 'em quick and easy. Make it clear what you write so that you can filter out the folks who won't like your stuff.

Part of that ties into your booth. The first time you go out to sell, your "stuff" consists of a tablecloth, an email list sign-up, and your product. Get out there, and just see how things go. Look at other booths around you and take notes. Figure out what you like and what you don't like. See what you can easily whip together to make your booth stand out more next time.

Then, each time you set up to sell at an event, add, remove, and tweak things a little. Just keep after it until you find that perfect setup that looks professional, but not too busy. If you do it correctly, your general look will quickly filter your target market for you!

My booth usually has some form of animal skull on it, made up to look creepy and occult. I have a little fake dead tree that I put a Mothman doll I bought in. Things like that, coupled with a black tablecloth and my book covers, do a good job of sending the message of "Hey, this guy writes weird occult-type stuff," and folks who like weird occult-type stuff are exactly my target market. If I see someone look at my booth and their lip curls or they look uncomfortable, I can just save my breath and talk to the next person to walk by.

And that is the single best thing I learned from Ben: Talk to everyone who walks by. Ideally, ask them a question. "Hey, do you like to read?" is a great filtering question. See someone walking by who looks like they might just pass by without marveling at your artistry? Ask them that. They will either say no, in which case you just say "No worries" or the like, or they will say yes. Then you get to ask them what they like to read, or maybe you ask if you can tell them a little about your book. If they say no, just thank them and move on.

Don't be pushy. No one likes pushy.

Ideally, try to vend alongside other authors whenever possible, especially at conventions. Having multiple authors of different but related genres at one table means you can pull in a wider selection of potential customers. It really does work great!

Time for an example!

A couple of years ago, Ben invited me to share a table with him and a few other authors at Atlanta Comic Con. Then, for some reason, that event folded into Fandemic, which is a *Walking Dead* fan convention.

You may not know much about me, but I didn't write *The Walking Dead*.

I don't even have zombies in my books. None of the authors in our booth did.

So, imagine, if you will, four authors (two UF, one dystopian sci-fi, one high fantasy) at an event now geared toward zombie/horror lovers. Now imagine our table being placed on the very outskirts of the vendor hall, quite a ways from the entrance. All in all, it was a recipe for a disaster. We had all sunk a decent chunk of change on this booth, and things looked bleak at first.

And yet, I managed to come just one book sale shy of breaking even. I didn't make any money, but I didn't lose much at all (fifteen bucks) and I know I generated a lot of connections, so the weekend was a net gain for sure. And the only reason why was because the four of us had worked together and had a variety on offer.

Anyone who walked by got asked if they liked books. If they said yes, they got asked what kind, and we then directed them to whichever author's works were the closest match. But you know what? Almost every single person then went on to ask all four of us about our books. And more often than not, they ended up buying books from someone that they didn't come over specifically to see.

Having a variety of products makes you appeal to a wider variety of folks. That's why I'm not just an UF author. I have horror, fantasy, steampunk, and South-ern Gothic works all in various stages of life, and one day all of them will grace my table so I will be able to lure in all of my fellow nerds with my siren call of printed words!

I've seen some other great options outside the realm of books too. Ben also carves fountain pens that he sells at his booth. Another author I know sells hand-carved little book props for your thumbs. A lot of authors sell bookmarks.

My last tip concerns pricing. Always, always, always have something cheap for sale. The lowest price on my books is fifteen dollars, but you know what? Not everyone has fifteen dollars, or wants to spend fifteen dollars on a book they might not read. But a lot of folks like to support, and if you give them a cheap option to support you, they will. Me, I sell stickers and postcards.

The postcards sell like ice cubes to arctic explorers, and the stickers sell like ice cubes to people in the Sahara. It's not uncommon for me to sell a hundred dollars' worth of stickers in a few hours. And this is money that, had I not had something cheap available on my table, I would likely have never seen! And an extra hundred bucks a day?

That's huge.

Just Ask

One of the biggest tips I ever got that has since become a bit of a gospel to me is to *just ask*. Wonder if you could be a panelist at a convention? Ask. Want to know if you can set up at that event? Ask. Curious if you could steal ten minutes of time from an author to ask them some questions? Ask.

Seriously. Just ask.

Here are some examples from my life!

I have gradually been doing more workshops and speaking-type engagements. It's an area I really want to buff up my resume on, partly because I like teaching folks about what I do, and partly because these things often will pay me. Getting paid to run my mouth about my passion? Yes, please.

So, one day I got an email from a publishing conference that I used to attend back before the Covid times. They were advertising for their upcoming event, and I thought to myself, "Hey, I wonder if they would let me speak?" So, I reached out—explaining who I was and my connection to the event—and linked my Convention/Speaking Resume page on my website. I explained that I was sure they were probably already full on speakers for this year, but when next year rolled around, I hoped to be considered.

I got an email back inviting me to be a paid speaker at that event, plus the sister event taking place in a different city the next day. All I did was ask.

Here's another example: One year I set a goal of being a panelist on six panels at Dragon Con. I knew Nancy and Venessa on the Writers' Track, but beyond that I didn't really know anyone who made those kinds of calls. So, guess what I did? I started asking.

I found out where the Digital Media Track held their discussions on panels, and I asked if I could do a "Podcasting for Authors" panel. They said yes. Then I saw their list of other panels they were looking at doing, and I asked if I could jump on a couple of others. Again, they said yes. I then reached out to the Urban Fantasy Track and asked if there was room for me—and they said no, but that's ok. Next, I reached out to the Table-top Gaming Track and asked if I could do a panel on one-sheet RPGs. Yet again, they said yes. Then they asked if I wanted to be on a panel about small board games, to which *I* said yes.

Boom. Six panels.

All because I asked.

Folks will tell you no, of course, and probably a lot more times than they'll say yes. That's just life. But no one has ever been mean to me for asking. I'm always polite, and I just throw myself out as a possible solution to a problem they may have. And these days, I tend to get more yeses than noes because I've put myself out there enough times that I've managed to cobble together a decent resume to fall back on.

Whenever I do a speaking engagement or workshop, I always end by saying that folks are welcome to go to my website and reach out to me via my contact form or hit me up on social media. A lot of times, no one will take me up on that, or maybe just one or two people. Maybe I'm a shit speaker—or maybe I'm so good, I answer every possible question. I know which of those my money is on.

But honestly, I'm a pretty good speaker; folks are just hesitant to ask, to follow up. And I get it! Throwing yourself out there is hard.

But seriously. Just ask.

It will be ok. And eventually, it will pay off in a big way.

Defining Success

I've always made a point of measuring success in my own way. For a lot of writers, anything short of getting traditionally published and writing for a living is failure. I've been more realistic, I feel, accepting that it's unlikely that I will ever reach those storied heights. I have been traditionally published in the past and will be again in the future (a horror novel of mine is being published by Falstaff Books as you read this—hell, maybe it's even out now!), but doing this full-time . . . I mean, have you seen American healthcare costs?

So, I have always used different goalposts to establish what success might look like for me personally. Usually, it's in the context of my next goal. For example, for a couple of years I thought success for me would be getting to do a panel at Dragon Con, which I achieved! And the following year, I was on six—one of which was with Sherrilyn Kenyon! (I know I said this earlier, but damn it, this was big for me!) And now, the following year, I was an official Attending Professional there!

Now, of course, the overall goal is to make a decent amount of money doing this. Ideally a livable amount, but though that would be nice, my perhaps more realistic goal is to make enough to be able to afford to be debt-free and travel more. I prefer experiences to things, so for me, "success" means getting my career to a point that I can travel wherever I want (within reason) whenever I want (also within reason). Since my day job gives me a nice chunk of vacation time, enough that I could be traveling a good bit, the real deal-breaker will be making more money.

But it's one thing to say "success is making enough money to go to New Zealand any year I want to go" and an entirely different thing to have some sort of road map leading you to that point. There are a lot of steps between "living paycheck to paycheck with no books published" and "world traveler."

And to me, here's the key: Every one of those steps is a victory. It's a new level of success. It's not the ultimate "success," sure, but each of them is still a success, so treat them that way!

Here's my method: I like to think of these in tiers. I make a list of shorter-term goals and a list of longer-term goals. Once I tick all the boxes in my shorter-term goals list, I have leveled up, and it's time to start working to tick all the boxes in my longer-term goals list. And once I do that, I make the next list! Eventually, if I achieve all my dreams, the last tier is going to have just one item on it: "Do this full-time."

Let me give you an example of my current two lists.

Here are my current short-term goals, with the bold items being ones I have completed at the time of writing this:

1. **Get 100 reviews on a book.**

2. **Do six panels at Dragon Con.**

3. **Sell 1,000 books.**

4. **100,000 KENP read.**

5. Have a $1,000 book launch.

6. **Have a $1,000 month in a non-launch month.**

7. Sell 5,000 books.

8. **Instagram over 500 likes.**

9. Facebook over 1,000 follows.

10. **250 subscribers to my email list.**

11. **Four Patreon patrons.**

For my longer-term goals, I have the following:

1. Sell 10,000 books.

2. Sell 50,000 books.

3. Sell 100,000 books.

4. **Traditionally publish a novel.**

5. **Make $10,000 in one year.**

6. Make $50,000 in one year.

7. Instagram and Facebook over 5,000 combined followers.

8. 1,000 reviews on a book.

9. Get over 100 reviews on at least 10 books.

10. Get an agent.

11. **Write a script and shop it around.**

12. 1,000 subscribers to my email list.

13. 5,000 subscribers to my email list.

I feel like the short-term goals set me up nicely to really start expanding and growing my author brand, and fulfilling all of the second list will have me just where I want to be: to be able to see the world with the LadyWife! And that, to me, is the very definition of success.

But you know what else I do? Every time I tick a box, I write a blog post to celebrate it. Because it really is a cause for celebration—I set a goal, I defined a marker for success, and I hit it! You should be doing the same thing!

Give yourself some easy wins to help build momentum. If your long-term goal is to write a novel, why not set a goal to write a short story to completion? And when you do, celebrate that fact! You achieved a goal, instead of just lazing about dreaming about what might could be!

In America, "success" is usually defined as being rich and/or famous. But for a lot of folks, that's not what success is. What success means to you will likely look very different from what it means to me, and that's amazing! So, figure out what you really want, start actually mapping out some goals to get there, and then celebrate the hell out of them once you achieve them! That's the most important part. Because if you don't sing your praises, odds are no one else will either!

Now let's get heavy for a second.

Reality Check

Like I said in the last chapter, I have always defined success in my own ways, which usually do *not* involve getting rich. For example, one pit stop on my road map to success was being on a panel at Dragon Con, which earns you exactly zero dollars. But for me, it was a goal I had been working and networking toward for years!

But behind it all, there is lurking a fear of mine: that I may keep after this whole writing thing for twenty or thirty years and essentially have nothing lasting creatively to show for it.

Now, I am lucky in that I have a decent day job, at least, so it won't be the case that I'm some all-around abject failure. I love and am loved, which is the most important part of life. But it could be that after decades of seriously pursuing my craft, I might have "nothing to show for it," by which I take to mean not having built any sort of lasting legacy that would survive my death.

I've never been under any illusions that I would be the next Stephen King, Robin Hobb, or Glen Cook. I've never thought that I would become a rich man off my craft. But . . . I'd be lying if I said I didn't envision a certain level of notoriety. The kind of person who might maybe have a series successful enough that the rights are bought by some movie studio to remain in production hell for a decade before inevitably reverting back to me, or the kind of person who could actually sell his autograph at a convention one day. I'm not saying I want to be Jim Butcher; I just want to be Jim Butcher-level famous, lol.

As an indie author, though, that is a tall, tall, *tall* order.

I've been doing this for a bit over a decade now. And sometimes I wonder, where will I be in ten years? Will I be some faceless author, toiling away in the mire for book launches that number, at most, a couple hundred sales? Or will I be a recognizable author who attends Dragon Con not as an Attending Professional, but as an invited Guest? Will the pilot script of my Jubal County Saga actually get optioned? Or will it just keep making the rounds to disinterested production companies?

I write because I love it, and I will continue doing so at the end of twenty years no matter the outcome. But I would love to have *my moment*, where I get to see the decades of work pay off in a big, tangible way. That's all. When I'm lying there on my deathbed from a Spam-induced heart attack, it would be cool to have a moment like that to look back on.

A boy can dream, right?

But that is what it is—a dream. And the horrible reality is, most of us will never get fully to where we want to be. Think about how many struggling artists, writers, musicians, and actors there are out there. We can't all make it big one day. We won't all be successes like we are in our dreams at night.

You can do everything in this book, and do it a million times better than me, and still not make it to your goal, because there is simply too much outside of our control. We don't control the economy. We don't control pandemics. We can't make people look at our ads or buy our products. We are vulnerable to the whims of the world at large, and the world is hard (that's what she said).

When I first started writing, I thought that doing this full-time was fairly easily achievable, if you had enough drive. But the longer I keep at this, the more I realize that drive is the engine that will take you to the opportunities that will make you a success—but it won't guarantee those opportunities will actually show up.

The sooner you face that fact, the better off you will be. Because then you can start to figure out what your fallback plan is. For me, once I realized the true state of what it means to get older and require health insurance, I knew that doing this full-time was—at best—going to take a decade longer than I would've liked, and there was every chance that day would never actually come.

So, I sat and thought about what would make me happy. And I decided that getting to travel more with my LadyWife was it, and that was something I could achieve. A couple of years to get us both totally out of debt, and then all this money coming in can go toward plane tickets and street food in foreign lands.

I'm sorry I can't promise you success. Life sucks like that. And I genuinely hope you are one of those overnight successes that I turn green with envy over! Really. I hope you get to exactly where you want to be; I just want you to be ready if it doesn't happen. Because odds are, even with this wildly exceptional book in your hand, it won't.

And that's ok.

Section Two: Find Other Revenue Streams

Man, it got heavy there for a second. So, let's get back on our bullshit and talk about the most important thing of all: making money! Right?

Getting the Ball Rolling

You want to be a rock star? Famous graphic artist? Filmmaker? Well, odds are, you're not going to hit a home run your first time out the gate. You might—and if so, I hate you, you lucky bastard. But until you do manage to hit it big, or at least reach your goal, you're going to need to find other ways to make money.

My big goal, of course, is to be a full-time writer of fiction. I am not there yet—not even all that close, really (damn you, my need for health insurance!). In the interim, though, I make a little money on the side in a number of ways. For example, for a long time I got paid to write a weekly blog post for a vape company in Florida. It didn't pay much, but it took practically no time and every little bit helps. I also had an account on Fiverr, where you could hire me to write you five hundred words of anything you wanted (if I were writing this for my Fiverr, I would have already made, like, a *lot* of bucks). I still do press work on occasion for a band I used to roadie for. I sell shirts I've designed on Amazon.

Those little dribs and drabs add up, and they're helping me to get my family of debt. Once we're totally out of debt, then I'll be that much closer to quitting my day job to write full-time. So, always be looking for ways to take your skill and make money off it. Fiverr is great for that, but let's say you are an artist. You aren't ready for your first gallery show, but those bills won't pay themselves. Maybe you go online and offer lessons, or set up a booth doing caricatures. It's not exactly what you *want* to be doing, but you'll be getting paid to do what you love instead of just sitting in your room wishing the power company would take a painting of a hundred-dollar bill as payment (spoiler: they won't).

Perhaps even more important than the money these little side ventures have given me, and will give you, is experience. I have written thousands of words for paying customers now, and if you think they just let things slide, well, you would be incorrect. In that way, I was able to hone my writing craft. For example, I am very well aware of how many times I've used variations of the word "create" over the course of this little book—far too many. Some Fiverr client would be pissed.

Learning what not to do is not the same as not doing it, clearly, or I would already have my millions! That's a whole other book I don't intend to write. Probably one that'll make someone else a lot of money, too, knowing my luck.

But also, don't be afraid to look at related fields. I enjoy writing Lovecraftian-style horror on occasion, and I hope to draw in fans who love the same. So, with the advent of drop-shipping companies like Amazon Merch/TeePublic, I've been able to launch a line of shirts related to a genre I love and that should appeal to my fans. Even if I only sell a few shirts a month, that gets me a few dollars closer to my dream, for a virtually zero-time investment beyond setup.

A word of warning, though: Don't let these new revenue streams consume you to the point you lose sight of what you really want. For example, I could have made a lot more money on Fiverr, but I turned down a number of large jobs because I realized it would take away too much time from my own personal writing. Eventually, I shut it down completely, as I moved more into connection-based freelancing that was better suited to my schedule. But hell, who knows? You might find out that the side venture you started is what you love doing the most, and you never knew until you tried it. Life can be funny like that.

So, let's dive into my side hustles' side hustles! Just understand that I'm not telling you each of these things so you can go out and replicate them exactly. These are examples designed to get you thinking about how *you* can do things that make sense for *your* very specific set of circumstances.

Book Sales

I'm an author! You may have picked up on this fact by this point in the book. If not, well . . . maybe you should consider being just a touch more observant.

Unsurprisingly, as an author, my number one focus is always selling books. That is the single most important element of the Tales by Bob Empire such as it is, and that is where the bulk of my focus goes. Because damn it, the goal is to be an author full-time, and word of mouth is the best marketing you can have. But if folks haven't read my books, then they can't be out there *wording* from their *mouths.*

So while I am about to tell you a bunch of other ways I make money, just understand that my goal each month is for the bulk of my money to come from selling books. Did it happen at first? God, no. It honestly took a long time to get to the point where I was selling more books than my combined other streams of revenue (and that was a damn low hurdle). But with a lot of luck and hard work, it's come to fruition.

How do I sell those books? Two ways.

The first way is, of course, online. The biggest market is obviously where the most people are, so that's where I have to sell my books. At the time of this writing, I'm exclusive to Amazon with my fiction, but since they're the biggest book market at the moment, I've been ok with being exclusive. Long-term, I plan to "go wide" with all of my physical books, but I only have so many spoons, and I just haven't taken that plunge yet. This book you're holding is actually the first book I have published wide.

Anyhoo, Kindle Unlimited is a fantastic way to build up your number of reviews, or at least it has been for me. I really hope I'm not telling you something you don't know when I say that's fucking invaluable. No, really! Selling books is hard, but selling books with no reviews is even harder.

So selling books online is good income, and I know a lot of authors for whom that is their primary form of sales. It's a good method. A *great* method. But it's also very time-consuming, so don't think you're going to be able to just throw your book up on Amazon and folks will find it and buy it organically—not gonna happen. So, you will need to market—and market *heavily*—to get noticed.

This is not a marketing guidebook, though, so we're just going to skip that aspect for now. Just know that you're going to have to market, and you should go talk with other authors about how they do it. Or go check out my blog and see what I post on there about it! I'm no whiz, though, so trust there are many better people to ask.

The other way I sell books, and by far my favorite way, is in person. At this point in my career, that is the single biggest moneymaker for me. Earning several hundred dollars in a single day? Yeah, I've not really *ever* done that online except during a book launch week. Even better, I get to talk—face-to-face, in person—to other booklovers while I do it. I get to make real connections and gather up fans like Pokémon. It's great!

Obviously I sell a lot at conventions, but not as much as you would think! The problem with conventions, for me, is that I'm always off doing a bunch of panels as a guest—which, to be clear, I love more than life itself. But if I'm out on a panel, that means I'm not working my booth and luring people in to sell them books with my dulcet cries of "meth wizard books." And really, you are your own best salesperson! So being there 100% helps tremendously.

Where I actually end up selling a lot more ends up being craft fairs and art markets. These types of events usually have fewer authors on-site, so I stand out a little bit more. I'm usually one of the few writing genre fiction, and certainly the only one writing meth wizard books, so then I stand out that much more. These are the events where I make the most per hour usually, especially when you factor in that usually I don't have to get a hotel room, travel very far, or pay a huge table fee. That's a win/win/win for me usually.

Even so, let's be real: Some events are just not going to go your way. You might have an event where you only sell one or two books, or sell just one print of a painting. Just remember, one bad event isn't a cause for worry. Now, if you have several in a row, then maybe you need to take a good, hard look at what you're doing. Is your table inviting? Does it look professional? Do you need to work on your elevator pitch? Are you actively engaging with passersby, or just sitting there on your phone?

Long story short: Whatever your main focus is career-wise needs to ALWAYS be your main focus income-wise. The rest of the income streams are nice, but they won't get you where you want to be, at least not on their own.

Freelancing

One day on Reddit, I happened to mention in a comment a bit about how I used freelancing to build up my publishing war chest. It drew some interest, so I wrote it up in more detail. As you'll see, I didn't set out to do this; I sort of blundered my way into it, but I'm happy with how it played out. So, take what I did, be more intentional with it, and it should (in theory) work even better for you.

My first experience with freelance writing was in the music industry. For a time (2008–2011ish), I made money doing freelance press work for bands and recording artists. I kept it up off and on up until 2019 or so, but those early years were when I was much more involved in the industry, so once I moved on from that, the work quickly dwindled until my only gigs were occasional ones for friends. It never paid super great, but I was poor, and I liked to eat. It was also good experience.

I began my actual writing journey late 2012. As the years passed, I shifted from getting my short stories placed into anthologies to working on longer works, like novellas and novels. When I made this shift, there was a large window of time where I was working on books and not really publishing anything. Initially, I hadn't really decided on self-publishing.

I was, however, still quite poor. And so I started doing freelance writing on Fiverr. My first go round, I kept it simple: for five bucks, I would write five hundred words of whatever someone wanted. I actually worked my way to being a "Level 2" seller by doing this (which isn't super easy). Here are some highlights of what I was asked to write:

1. A gritty crime noir story about a person's pet cat.

2. A *Doctor Who/My Little Pony* crossover erotica.

3. A large amount of smut, especially cyborg related.

4. Long lists of potential magical items for a game someone was working on.

I actually ended up turning down quite a large amount of work. I had several folks reach out to me to see if I would ghostwrite a book for them, or even (in one case) a series of books. I was actually able to determine who one of them was, and they were a self-published author with a large number of books out. In every case, I turned down any gig longer than five thousand words, pretty much. At that point, I didn't have a novel of my own out, and I was gonna be damned if my first published novel wasn't under my own name.

All told, I made a few grand doing it. Much of that went to just living, but a fair chunk went to business-type expenses. Microphones, a laptop, that sort of stuff. It was a pretty good gig, and the money certainly helped. It was also great experience, as I ended up writing in a lot of genres that I normally would not have. I got to stretch my authorial legs a bit, and it gave me more practice on writing to a deadline (building on what NaNoWriMo had already done for me).

In the end, though, I stopped. I was somewhat a victim of my own success, as the more gigs you complete, the more you get shown in the search results, which means the more folks end up hiring you. I reached a point where I was spending more time writing for other people than myself, and once I realized that, I shut it down. I actually deleted my account (which you cannot get back) to remove the temptation.

So, some time passed. I started to get more and more serious about treating things like a business, and I had started doing some things like designing some shirts to throw up on Amazon POD. I was getting a small amount of passive income coming in, but nothing at all to write home about. Talking under a hundred bucks a month.

I ended up talking with the guy I now consider my mentor, John G. Hartness, and he convinced me to go self-pub with my main series. This was not all that long before Covid came along. In conjunction with this, I was getting more and more into the indie tabletop RPG design space. I fell in love with one-sheet RPGs and started making them as a hobby.

So, I could see where I was going to have some expenses coming up. I also was entertaining the idea that it might be nice to really explore the idea of being an actual full-blown game writer. Mostly the latter, if I'm being honest, as at this point I didn't have a full vision of just what self-publishing was going to cost to do properly. Anyhoo, these two ideas merged together, and I decided to get back on Fiverr.

I set up a new account (couldn't get my old one back, remember?), and this time I went a bit more niche. I said for five bucks, I "will write or world-build for your video or tabletop game." At that time, I was pretty much the only person really doing that. Now I search and there are a bunch more, though at least at a quick glance, as of this writing I still have the most reviews.

I set out with the goal of making some money, but also building up my credits. I wanted to build a resume I could use to potentially get jobs with the sorts of companies that don't hire strangers off Fiverr for their needs. So, I only took jobs that I was allowed to take credit for having written on. If I couldn't claim it on my website, then I wasn't interested. I also turned down a fair number of gigs over ethical issues. Many, many people would reach out to get even more world-building done for their novel or game, and

I quite often would tell them that they already had more than enough material, explained world-builder's disease to them, and sent them on their way in hopes that they would stop world-building and start writing. Because I've been there before in the past myself.

I also ended up getting hired by several NFT companies before I realized what they were. Once I understood what they actually were, I stopped taking work from them.

I did it pretty hard and heavy for a couple of years, whenever I had free time. I also increased my fee to ten bucks per five hundred words to make it more worth my time. I can crank out a thousand words an hour pretty consistently, and $20/hour was a lot more than what I was making per hour at my day job at the time. I was more careful to make sure I didn't allow it to overtake my primary writing time on my personal works, which I did a good job of. It was also a lot of fun. This is my favorite type of writing, really, and if it was more profitable, it might have ended up becoming my focus. I ended up stopping (though this time I kept my account open, haha) because my books were starting to come out. Once they were out, the time I spent freelancing was converted into marketing time, essentially.

Anyway, I made over three grand. Coupled with passively selling my shirts, indie RPGs, and all that sort of stuff, I had all the money I needed to hire my editors, cover designer, and buy needed software. Since it took until around book four for me to fully break even on launch costs, it was nice to not have to come out of pocket on any of those expenses. For years now, I've been keeping all of my profits going into a separate bank account (even though I am a sole proprietorship), and I use that pile for all my expenses.

So, that's how I built up my publishing war chest before I ever put out my first book.

To fully round out the education, here's a lot of more exact info about my more recent Fiverr adventure.

135 reviews, 5 stars.

$3,111.52 in earnings.

And here is what my actual pitch on there read:

DO NOT HIRE ME WITHOUT TALKING TO ME FIRST TO MAKE SURE I AM A GOOD FIT FOR YOUR PROJECT. I STRONGLY encourage you to message me first with the scope of your project, so that I can make sure we are on the same page about expectations, and that your project is within my abilities/availability.

For this gig, I will craft you 500 words of what it is your game needs. Need flavor text for item drops? How about lore for your characters? Maybe descriptions of countries for your players to visit? Whatever you can come up with, I can flesh it out and put it to paper. I can do dialogue, map story arcs, or brainstorm classes and mechanics. I can crank out histories, plot hooks, and character ideas. If it's written and has to do with some form of gaming, odds are I have written something similar in the past and am thus at least somewhat experienced with your specific needs.

As for my qualifications, I am a published author who has been playing computer and console games for over 25 years now, and tabletop games like DnD for over 15 years. I have also written for multiple published apps/games, have released a number of TTRPGs, and created numerous worlds for game and story concepts.

Hope this helps.

Shirts

Look, there are a few ways you can go about this. One path involves getting a screen printer to make a bunch of shirts yourself. But then you have to carry inventory, and decide how many of what size to make in what color, and . . . ugh. It's a lot. You'll make good money per shirt, though.

I opted to go a much cheaper way that earns a lot less money: POD shirts. Print on demand means you just upload your design, and when someone orders it, the company prints and ships it. That way, you don't have to worry about inventory, shipping, or any of that mess. However . . . you don't make much. For example, my designs on TeePublic get me about two bucks a shirt sale. If I were printing and selling them myself, that might be ten bucks or more.

But I just don't have the time or energy to manage all that. The cut in pay is certainly worth it for me. You may decide differently, and that's ok. Do what makes sense for you.

Just keep these things in mind:

- If making shirts isn't your main hustle, then

you don't want to spend more time dealing with shirts than writing books, painting, etc.

- Where possible, reuse deigns. For example, I took parts of my book covers and turned them into shirts. Two products for the price of one, sorta.

- Learning the basics of graphic design is not that hard and will save you a ton of money. I recommend using Affinity Designer. Again, fuck Adobe and its pay-per-month model.

So yeah, shirts can be a tidy little amount added to your income if you want to check it out.

Simple RPGS

I love role-playing games. They have been a passion of mine for decades now, and once I started applying the self-publishing mindset to my hobby and learned about the indie RPG space . . . well, making my own games was a natural fit. At the time of writing this, I've made something like thirty-five games of varying complexity, from one-sheet games to more lengthy ten-plus page entries. I take these games, make them into PDFs, whip up a terrible cover, and then put them up on sites like itch.io and DriveThruRPG. And lately, I've started actually taking my best ideas and turning them into printed twenty-pages zines.

Do they make much money? Hell no.

Were they fun to make? Hell yes!

Would I have made them anyway? Probably. Again, this is a hobby first for me.

Should you rush out right now to make a bunch of simple RPGs to sell? Almost certainly not.

I share this for two reasons: First is completeness. I want to paint a picture for you of all the things I get up to. You need to make informed choices, and if you're using this book to help make them, I want you to understand exactly where I'm coming from.

Secondly, this is just an example. You have a hobby or passion—figure out if there's a quick and easy way for you to potentially monetize it, even in a small way, to help fund your eventual goals. Maybe you like to knit as a hobby. If so, why not knit up a little creature from your books to have for sale at your table?

Those are the kinds of things I'm hoping this book will get you to think about.

Patreon

Let's talk subscription services. Patreon is one of those sites where your fans and audience can directly support you on a recurring basis. It doesn't have to be Patreon that you use specifically; it could be Ko-fi, OnlyFans, or whatever. I use Patreon because that's what I came across first that made sense to me. It's been a very slow build, but over time I've worked up to having about a dozen "patrons." Each month, I get a small sum of money from Patreon because of it.

What do I share there for my patrons? That's the brilliant part: it's all stuff I would already be doing anyway! Right now on my Patreon, you can get:

1. Every short story I've published in anthologies that I have regained the rights to.

2. A bunch of fun flash fiction.

3. A number of essays written in the voice of Howard Marsh, my redneck wizard, talking about . . . well, whatever is on his mind. It gets wild.

4. Sneak peaks at my book covers before anyone else.

5. Big news that I break there first, like about my audiobooks coming out.

6. Draft chapters from my books.

You could easily be doing the same. The hard part is just being consistent with it. It took me a long time, but I've now finally gotten good about putting up new content on there every week. Once I started doing that, I started slowly but consistently gaining followers.

Affiliate Links

This is sort of a no-brainer: Go to Amazon and sign up for their affiliate program. Read all the rules. Make sure your website and social media accounts are connected to it. Now, use those links. Did you review a book on your blog? Put a link to the book in the post and use your affiliate link!

It's that simple. You won't get rich off it, but one time I had someone use my link and then go buy an air conditioner, and I got a couple hundred bucks from it!

Most months I make under two bucks, though . . . so maybe moderate your expectations a bit.

Getting Paid for My Presence!

Somehow, along the way, folks started paying for me to be at a place. I'm as befuddled as you are.

Well, not really, I guess—I have worked pretty fucking hard to network and build up my credentials over the past few years, and that has begun to pay off. It started slow, with a super small convention in South Alabama paying me to be their guest of honor. Which, if I'm the guest of honor, that should give you an idea of just how "big" that convention was. But by god, I *have* been a guest of honor, and if you don't think that has been added to my resume, you're not paying attention!

I also started giving some free workshops to local writing groups and at libraries. This let me hone my presentations and learn how to work a very different sort of crowd. And when you're asking to be a presenter at an event, it's excellent to be able to say, "Hey, I presented this panel at XXXX Literary Event." The folks you're applying to aren't going to ask you for a copy of the invoice; they'll never know that it was unpaid unless you tell them.

And in turn, all that has grown to the point where this year (2024), I've now actually been *paid* to teach workshops at three different events, and I have at least one more to do before the year is up. Some pay room, board, and travel; others just pay for the class time, but all of them pay me at least a couple hundred bucks. And as an added bonus, I usually sell a few books there too.

You probably have or will develop some niche expertise. Start teaching it to your fellows for free, or at conventions, and then start asking if you can teach it for money.

"Just ask." —Bob, in this book, repeatedly

Section Three: Transparency

You've made it this far, so you're probably pretty damn aware that I'm a huge proponent of transparency. I enjoy it when a creative peels back the curtain and lays out all the numbers (which happens far too rarely), so I've long been sharing blog posts about how I did each month, how my book launches go, and the exact cost to get my books to market. This section will be like that, but more big picture. We're also going to take some time to talk about mental health and the like, so fair warning!

How Bob Still Isn't a Full-Time Author after a Decade(ish) of (Sorta) Working at It!

So, here it is—a fairly comprehensive history of how I came to be where I am now. Is it a roadmap you can follow? Sure. Maybe. Probably not . . . at least not exactly. Your journey will be your own, but I hope in reading this, you'll get a feel for how things change, how things grow, and how things could be.

I'm going to break my path along into sections. Each one will have a rough span of years beside the title, but there was rarely any sort of clean break between these stages. Most of these sections will in some ways overlap with the next, so expect the dates to reflect that. Here we go:

Pre-Stage: I've Always Liked to Write

As far back as I can remember, I have liked to write. I have a copy of a book about a monster who killed people with a ham sandwich that I wrote in, like, first grade I think? I was called Lowa, which was AWOL backwards. Why that? No clue. I think the ham sandwich was a reference to . . . *Coach*? *Designing Women*? Some old TV show I saw around that time, anyway.

My first attempt to write anything serious was a try at writing a Warhammer novel when I was in high school. It went poorly, being little more than dwarven wish fulfillment. Oof . . . I cringe to think about it even to this day. In high school, I also developed a habit of writing one-page flash fiction that were usually pun based. They would usually get a chuckle from my teachers.

In college, I tried my hand at writing some very gnostic-inspired eldritch horror. I don't think anything really survives from this time beyond some general world-building that wound up inspiring some of my Jubal County horror-related stories.

In 2008, I got divorced and laid off within a few months of each other. With suddenly a lot more free time on my hands, I tried my hand at writing another novel, this time a fantasy book set in a world I had created for DnD. I think I got four or five chapters done at most before fizzling out. I also sporadically wrote the odd mopey sadboi poem over the next decade or so. But after this failed novel, I don't think I wrote a single line of prose until late 2012. At least not one that wasn't directly tied to some DnD campaign I was running.

Stage One: The Short Stories of Robert McGough (2012–2015ish)

I started my "career" back in the fall of 2012 with the completion of my first NaNoWriMo, in which I wrote fifty thousand words of short stories. I literally asked my friends how they would like to die in a short story, and then wrote them up. This was me knocking the dust off a passion I'd had when I was younger and had rediscovered as I was in the tail end of my master's program in a degree that had zero relation to writing.

Once I had these stories in hand—some fantasy, some horror, some steampunk, and a decent amount of quasi-Southern Gothic (where I was building the world of Jubal County without realizing it yet)—I decided that it was time to get out there and tackle the world! My very first piece got published in the Rubicon, the Troy University Literary Journal. They actually changed the rules to allow me to submit as an alumni, which I thought was really awesome of them. This led to me looking into other literary journals and the like, which is where my first few credits came from. Here's a list of what I got out there:

- "Gone Bad" – *The Rubicon*, Spring 2013, Troy University Literary Journal

- "We Serve At Seven" – *The Rubicon*, Fall 2014, Troy University Literary Journal

- "Stilton's Crossroads" – *Squawk Back Magazine*, Issue 140, April 2015

- "Toothsome" – *Weird Montgomery*, Vol. 1, Issue 6

While having some folks publish my Southern Gothic-ish stuff was nice (three of the four above are set in proto-Jubal County), my first loves have always been horror and fantasy. That is the stuff I really wanted published. Plus, I wanted to get paid (the above paid in copy, at most).

So, I started hitting Facebook groups that shared places you could submit to anthologies, and I began sending stories out. A lot of rejections came in, of course, mostly form letters. But I did get a few personalized rejections, which I cherished. And then, wonder of wonders, I got a few acceptances! I tacked every rejection and acceptance up on the wall above my work station, a sort of wall of inspiration.

And that's when I learned that short story anthologies, at least small-press indie sorts, pay absolutely terribly. I recall getting my one and only royalty check in the mail, and it was for four bucks and some change. Most of them paid maybe ten bucks plus an author copy. A few would let us buy copies at cost to then turn around and sell. But you know what? Folks don't usually have a ton of interest in buying a book that you only have one story in. Some do . . . but most don't.

That was when I realized that if I was going to one day hope to do this for a living, I was going to have to start writing novels. So, while I tried to decide what I was going to write, I kept on churning out steampunk and horror short stories. I actually developed a large number of steampunk stories during this time that were all interconnected, roughly telling the backstory of how a team of heroes came to be together in this fantasy steampunk world I had created.

Here are some of the collections I had stories placed in:

- "Whispers on the Wind" – *Journals of Horror: Found Fiction*, Horror Anthology Edited by Terry M. West, Released October 2014

- "Colonel Gurthwait and the Black Hydra" – *Avast, Ye Airships Anthology*, Edited by Rie Rose Sheridan, Released February 26th 2015

- "The Jar" – *Southern Haunts: Magick Beneath the Moonlight*, Edited by Seventh Star Press, Released November 2015

- "Black Dog" – *New Legends: Caster, Castle, Creature*, Edited by Visual Adjectives Press, Released May 2016

Stage Two: My First Brush with Traditional Publishing (2015ish–2017)

Not too terribly long after I got good and rolling along in my writing, I was approached by a small traditional academic press. Essentially, they knew I had been a part of a writing group on campus and could take criticism well. And since I was writing steampunk, a genre they wanted to break into by starting an imprint for, they offered to publish collections of my short fiction. The plan was to release four small e-books of around twenty-five thousand words each, spread out over a couple of years. At the time we entered into the agreement, I had three of the four totally written, and I had the last one written as the third came out.

This certainly stoked the ego—but I never made any money from them. Not a cent. They paid out every quarter that you made at least fifty dollars. When you consider that Amazon was taking 35% and the press was taking 35%, there wasn't a ton of % left for me. Which still could have worked, if:

- 1. They had done any sort of real promotion. But they were new to this type of publishing and didn't know the right moves to take.

- 2. They had actually edited all of the three books they put out (they ended up releasing an entire volume unedited).

- 3. I had known anything about marketing and felt comfortable promoting them myself (I refused to promote an unedited book—I was ashamed of it).

All in all, it wasn't a great experience. It did stoke the ego, which was nice, sure. But it made no money, and in the end I had a product I was ashamed of being associated with. So, we agreed to go our separate ways. I don't hold them any real animus; that was their first foray into genre fiction publishing, which they were unprepared for, and I didn't do my due diligence either. Not that I knew what my due diligence would have been—at this point, I had never met another non-academic author, so I had no one to talk to about it.

Here's what I ended up getting published through them:

- "Rumor Has It" – Released August 2015

- "Red Sky at Morning" – Released August 2016

- "Within the Siren's Call" – Released October 2017

Stage Three: Writing, but to What Purpose? (2016–2018)

All the while, I kept writing. I churned out a ton more horror short stories. I started work on a steampunk novel set in my fantasy steampunk setting, but it fizzled. I wrote a small self-help book called Create Your Way to Freedom (which I sold for a bit, and which you now hold a much expanded and updated version of). I played around in some other settings and started working on the stuff that would become the first Jubal County novellas. I started writing some dark fantasy shorts in a new setting, called the Konislund. I started a writing group in my area at some point during all this, one that ran up until Covid hit.

Then I got hit with an idea for a horror novel: *Capitol of Nightmares.*

This novel was written pretty much in two months, with a two-year gap between them. I wrote the first half for NaNoWriMo one year, then two NaNos later I wrote the other half. I now had successfully finished my first full-length novel! I was pretty blown away at that fact, to be honest. And I wasn't really sure what to do next.

That's when I found out about these events where you can pay some money and they'll give you face time with actual agents you can pitch your book to. You also get some classes out of them, but I always skipped the classes for the most part and just did the pitch sessions. I ended up being asked to send in the first few chapters or fifty pages a few times, but no one ever signed me on. Which was pretty disheartening, but what can you do? I also tried sending it to a few agents once or twice, but I'll be honest, my heart wasn't in it.

You see, I had no idea if I was actually any good or not. I had no idea if I was just wasting my time. No one outside my friends and family had ever really read my work, so I had no validation. My adventure with the small press didn't inspire a lot of confidence, either, what with never even making the fifty bucks it required to get a payout.

I did end up having one friend read my novel, someone who surprised me by asking to do so; I was under the impression they weren't a big reader. And that friend loved it so much, they got *their* friends to read it! Which is honestly the only reason I tried the little bit that I did to shop it around.

So I was writing a lot of words, but to what end? I wasn't really seriously trying to get them published; I had even stopped submitting my short stories places for the most part. I was writing, sure . . . but nothing was getting me closer to my dream.

Step Four: Freelancing on Fiverr (2016–2017)

My memory isn't the best, so I'm not entirely sure what dates I started and stopped freelancing on Fiverr. But by this point you should have read all about that back in the Freelancing chapter. If not . . . why are you skipping around?

Anyway, why did I stop?

Because I was spending too much time writing other people's stuff. I found that I was prioritizing the work of others. Now, if my only goal was to be paid to write words for a living, then I could likely have kept working at that and maybe even eventually gotten there. But my dream is to be an author of my *own* books, and this got in the way of that.

Step Five: My First Brushes with Self-Publishing (2017–2019)

As I started winding down on Fiverr, I decided to dip my toes a little more seriously into self-publishing. In 2016, I had released the tiny little self-help book that eventually one day grew up to be what you are now holding, so I knew a bit about how to go about it. But a seven-thousand-word e-book (this version is well over four times larger—what a bargain!) that your friend traded you work for to get the cover made is one thing. Putting out something longer, though . . .

I decided to put out two collections of short stories, each around twenty-five thousand words. These were those dark fantasy short stories set in the Konislund. So, I decided to put out "The Tales of the Konislund" initially as two e-books, then as a bound single volume. And you know what? I did it.

And this is where I learned that if I am not confident in my product, I will not promote it. I still didn't know much about marketing, and I still wasn't sure if I could write worth a damn. And the editing was pretty damn slapdash. Then my neighbor left one of the e-books a one-star review and just really tore it to shreds.

If you hunt super hard, you may find some sort of vestige of these books on Amazon. I can assure you, I do not endorse you trying. They may be generally ok in content, but the editing was very subpar, and I am just super unhappy with them. So, I took them down, and one day you may see them again . . . but not anytime soon.

Stage Six: Getting Serious, and Becoming Bob (2017–2021)

I still knew that novels were most likely going to be what got me to where I wanted to be, and one horror novel does not a career make, so while I was dipping my toes into self-publishing I also tried my hand at writing another novel. What ended up happening was that I wrote two books, part one and two in a military fantasy series. *Bladeborn* and *Blightborn* are sitting in the chest, waiting for me to write *Gallowsborn* (if I can ever figure out what I want it to look like), and then they may see the light of day.

I also knew that for the most part, I was not happy with my work that was out to date. Well, I was actually fine with the anthologies I'd been in, but here's a weird tick of mine: I knew it was going to drive me up the wall to have all those anthologies showing on my Amazon Author page alongside my Jubal County Saga. I wanted folks to click my name and *only* see books that would actually generate me money. Those anthologies, I am proud of being in them, but more in a "list it on a resume or overly long blog post" sort of way and less of an "I want folks to go out and read them" sort of way. So, I stopped writing under Robert and started writing under Bob, which is what I go by in my day-to-day life anyway. Hence, Tales by Bob, not Tales by Robert.

To jump ahead just a tiny nudge, in 2020 I decided that I wanted to get some credits writing for video games or tabletop games. I have always been heavily invested in this space, being a Dungeons and Dragons player since 2004 or so, and once even toying with starting a d20 company. So, I started another Fiverr account where for five and later on ten bucks, I would do five hundred words of world-building or lore for your game.

When I started, I was the only person on there really doing it, and I got to work on a ton of cool projects. I only took projects that would allow me to credit myself as having worked on them, and it was a ton of fun! I ended up stopping about a year and a half later for basically the same reasons I stopped working on Fiverr the first time, but it was a fun ride while it lasted. It also served to build up my self-publishing war chest, which was honestly the best part, though I didn't realize it at the time!

At Dragon Con 2019, I saw that they had sign-ups to get a fifteen-minute mentor session with an author or publisher. I looked, and I saw the name John G. Hartness. While I hadn't heard of him, I saw that he had written a series called *Bubba the Monster Hunter*, which, when you're sitting on a collection of books about a redneck wizard, seems like the one person in all the world that would be perfect to talk to.

At this point, I really just had one question I desperately needed to be answered: Should I try to shop around this weird little redneck wizard novella series I had written, or would it be a waste of time? John seemed like the perfect person to talk to, and turns out, he was. He basically laid it out that traditional publishers don't typically like novellas, and that a methgician would be an even harder sell. But he explained that the very things that made it a bad fit for most traditional publishers made it a good fit for self-publishing, if I would take it seriously.

I left that Dragon Con feeling so energized. I had, at this point, done a few events at small conventions and libraries (Fanticon, SonoCon, and Gump City Comic Con). Not really seriously selling, but more along the lines of a promotional booth just pitching me and my podcasts (with the odd short story collection that I had a tale featured in) in exchange for doing organizing and moderating a few panels. But now, I was resolved: Get these books out, and do ALL THE CONS!

In February of 2020, I took my now LadyWife to our first con, a steampunk convention in Atlanta. We had a blast, and I was excited to really start hitting the ground running.

Covid, as you know, came in March.

And so my plans for doing a ton of conventions were promptly dashed. But seeing as I was spending my free time in my bubble now, mostly just curling up on couches with the LadyWife, I decided it was now or never. I learned what I could about self-publishing, hired an editor and a cover designer, and put out book one of the Jubal County Saga. My editor was British, and she "fixed" all my Southern dialect in the dialogue. My cover designer was Czech, and I found her on

Fiverr. She was fantastic. I paid them out of money I'd earned on Fiverr, so it didn't have to come out of pocket.

And, yeah, book one didn't sell well. For book two, I swapped editors (Cleo is from Texas, and she's fantastic—she edits everything of mine now) and taught myself enough graphic design that with my LadyWife helping me choose the colors (I'm shit at color selection), I was able to make my own cover. And you know what? It didn't sell well, either. It actually sold worse.

But I was such a baby writer still at that point that having a launch that made over a hundred bucks was a huge deal for me. The bigger deal, though, was that reviews started to come in from all the free e-book copies I had given away. And the reviews were good! Even better, they were good reviews from total strangers!

That was truly what I had needed most of all. The validation from strangers that I might not be the next Earnest Hemingway, but I was at least a solid writer that folks actually enjoyed to read.

Here's what I got out during this time:

- *Meteorology – Alabama's Emerging Writers –* Edited by Z Publishing, Released August 2018 (Under Robert, I believe)

- *The Essential Guidebook to the Secret Lives of Clams –* Released March 2020 (This is so dumb, but I love it. Total joke book, and released under Robert. It will see the light of day again, though!)

- *Bringing Home the Rain: The Redemption of Howard Marsh 1* – Released August 2021

- *The Depth Of The Water: The Redemption of Howard Marsh 2* – Released November 2021

I also did my first panel at a bigger con, Alabama Comic Con.

Stage Seven: The Other Hustles

I want to briefly acknowledge some of the things that I did/still do along the way that aren't author related, but are more brand related. I've long known that to reach my dream, having a bunch of revenue streams adding together would make my plan a lot more viable than just relying on book sales. I covered these more in-depth earlier, so you've read how they work, but this will put them in sequence for you. Here are some other side avenues:

- Very early on, I started doing freelance writing for bands. I still occasionally do it if the name is big enough or if they're a friend. I've written for artists like Stitches, Upchurch the Redneck, and Goldy lockS.

- I've had a Patreon since long before it made sense to have one; I don't even remember when I started it, to be honest. But at this point, I have about a dozen subscribers.

- In 2018, I started selling POD shirts on Amazon. I didn't put any real time into it until 2020, though, when I designed and listed about 150 new designs.

- In 2018, I started the Books, Beards, Booze podcast alongside a dear friend, and it's run off and on ever since. This makes essentially no money, but I think of it like backdoor advertising. In 2022, I started the Southern Fried Fantasy podcast, where I interview Southern authors. It has since been completed. Same deal, though—zero money.

- In 2020, I started making and releasing small, simple RPGs. Most are one-sheet RPGs, but a few have been longer. I sell them on itch.io and DriveThruRPG. After some time, I started turning the best ideas into full-length print zines.

Stage Eight: Starting to Make Real Progress (2021–Today)

In 2022, book three in my Jubal County Saga came out, and for the first time I broke even on a book launch. I realize making $450ish on a launch sounds like peanuts to some authors, but for me? Damn, that was huge! So, I decided to keep after it and get the rest of the first six books written and out there. And as of me writing this, they are all out into the world!

Outside getting the books to press, the biggest step forward for me has been networking with other authors. At the 2021 Dragon Con, I went to a panel that had another author self-publishing Southern urban fantasy. We swapped emails after, and that is how I met

Ben Meeks. We've vended, paneled, and brainstormed together countless times since. He's who introduced me to Venessa Giunta, who runs the only author group on Facebook worth a damn. Through them and John G. Hartness, I have met and gotten to network with so, so, so many great people who have become my con family.

I also got on a big transparency kick. It has long frustrated me that 99% of authors don't really talk about their number of sales/how much they make. This kind of secrecy made it impossible for me to tell if I was doing good, terrible, ok, or whatever, at least early on. Once I made friends with some other authors, sure, they would tell me in private how sales were, but that doesn't help folks looking to get into this space with real data. So, I started breaking all that kind of stuff down all the time, where anyone who wants to can read it.

So yeah, at this point I feel like I'm actually really starting to make some good headway. There are small steps back all the time, of course, but in general each year has been far better than the one before it. If I can just keep up that trajectory, then everything will be coming up Milhouse! Anyway, here's what I accomplished during this period:

- *Feet in the Fire: The Redemption of Howard Marsh 3* – Released January 2022

- *Praying the Day's Not Poison: The Redemption of Howard Marsh 4* – Released August 2022

- *Walking the Darkness Down: The Redemption of Howard Marsh 5* – Released March 2023

- *Calling the Devil Partner: The Redemption of Howard Marsh 6* – Released July 2023

- *Southern Saudade: A Supernatural Southern Gothic Collection* – Released October 2023

I've now done panels at: Dragon Con, CONjuration, Multiverse, ConCarolinas, more Alabama Comic Con, Fandemic, and Magic City Con. I was even the Author Guest of Honor at Imagicon!

I've also been a paid speaker at events like the Atlanta Self-Publishing Conference and the Alabama Writing Workshop.

Stage Nine: The Future

So, where am I headed? In short, it's now time to start getting a lot of the other items I've had in the chest out into the light. I want to be able to cater to a wider swath of readers by having horror, fantasy, and steampunk works available on my table and website. These are all genres I love and write already—I just need to get them out there for folks to read! I have also signed a book deal with Falstaff Dread, the horror imprint of Falstaff Books, to publish *Capitol of Nightmares*!

My goal has been to get to where I'm doing at least one convention or large festival each month. And that is pretty much the case now, with most months having multiple events. In-person sales will be a huge part of my career if I can get to that point, so laying that groundwork and building connections can never start too soon.

When I started back in 2012, I had set myself a ten-year goal of making my dream come true. But in reality, while I was putting in work the whole time, I really consider my journey to have started in earnest when I made the switch from Robert to Bob. So, my dream of dreams is that in about eight years, I will retire from my state job to do this full-time.

Will I get there? Eh, probably not. Mostly because health insurance is expensive, and it ain't gonna get any cheaper for my fat and aging ass. But will I try?

You bet your ass I will.

Here are a few other random date-based data points:

My author Facebook page was created on August 19, 2013.

Talesbybob.com was started on June 2, 2014.

My Instagram was created in February of 2017.

I began my Patreon in September of 2018, I believe.

My newsletter began on September of 2019. The landing page specifically was launched on September 29, 2019.

That September was also when I revamped my blog and began taking it much more earnestly.

My Struggle with Mental Health

Transparency is important to me, as you know by now, so I want to start by relaying my own struggles with mental health. Not as some cry for attention, but to help normalize discussions like this. There is zero shame in admitting you have an issue or need help. So, here we go, with a trigger warning for talk of suicide, depression, and self-harm:

As long as I can remember, I have been a bit of an odd duck. And there is absolutely nothing wrong with that—odd ducks make the world go round. But odd ducks have a . . . certain propensity for mental disorders. The vast majority go through their lives with nary a worry, but some fall through the cracks.

My crack came in the months and years after my divorce. I came to find I was singularly unprepared for rejection on that level. I have always had issues with rejection (child of divorce, yadda yadda), but this was an order of magnitude greater than anything I had ever experienced. I did not handle it well. Or at all, really.

During a more lucid moment, I made sure to remove the bullets from my house, which was good, as I went on to attempt suicide by cutting my wrists about a week later. Luckily I was unable to force myself to cut deep enough, but in the process I acquired a nasty habit: cutting. Any night that I didn't drink myself to sleep, I would slice myself a few times with a box blade.

I had a bit of a wake-up call when I cleaned up my room one day and removed over thirty empty bottles of liquor. That was when I severely cut back on my drinking, and for a number of years after, I would only ever drink at parties. This did nothing for the cutting, however, and when I lost my job a few months later, my depression worsened. It is really hard to motivate yourself to job hunt when you're depressed, so for those of my friends who have done just that, you are a rockstar.

I eventually moved back to the town where I got my undergraduate degree. I had rationalized to myself that my problem was that I needed a career and a girlfriend. If I had those two things, everything would be ok, and I was convinced going back to school would net me both. I had not yet realized a number of important things, the most important one being: Be ok with who you are. Other people will never make you happy if you cannot make yourself happy. Other people can always cheer you up, but deep-rooted happiness can only come from within.

Unsurprisingly, my depression worsened. I took to locking myself away in my room for weeks at a time, only coming out for work and class. I was a terror to be around when I wasn't locked away, and I knew it. I would buy my roommate things like video games to try and make up for what an ass I was being, rather than address the issue of being an ass. Because at that point, I couldn't; I had no idea what was wrong. I mean, I knew I was sad, but by that point I was long over my divorce. *Long* over. So why was I still sad?

I have a number of friends who know they have something wrong with them. And when this realization hits, invariably one of two things happens: they either get help and get better, or just stew in it and don't get better. I have yet to have a friend who had some sort of mental kerfuffle and then got better on their own. Some get worse, some stay the same, but no one gets better alone. So if you take nothing else from this, fucking listen to this right here:

Get help. It will change your life in ways you cannot even begin to understand right now.

The county I lived in had income-based mental health services, I found out. My income was well below poverty level, so I went. And it was amazing. It has changed my life for the better like nothing ever has. The seven or eight months I was able to go there helped me learn more about myself than the previous four or five years of introspection. I haven't cut even once since my third visit there. I've felt the urge a time or two, but I was given the tools to help resist.

I learned I am an introvert. You may scoff, having met me, but I really am. I just don't allow myself to act that way; there is simply too much I have to get done. But I have learned that I am, and I've also learned a number of coping mechanisms that have changed my life. Instead of being a forced extrovert, I am now an introvert who just throws himself out there, then runs home and detoxes from peopling for a few days. And it works! And yet . . .

The one mental kerfuffle I came out of there with, which I still struggle with, was being diagnosed with mild OCD-like tendencies. As I understand it, I don't have full-blown OCD—I just have certain traits in common with those who are.

As far back as I can remember, I have treated inanimate objects as though they were living. As though objects have emotions and feelings, and can be pleased or hurt or feel neglected. I'm told this comes from some sort of desire to exert control over my surroundings. So, every day, I try harder and harder to treat a spoon just like a spoon. Other people's things no longer bother me; it's just my own now. And it gets better. It's slow, but one day maybe I will get there. I have the toolkit my therapist equipped me with, and should it not prove up to rebuilding the scaffolding of my mind, then I'll go out there and find someone with the right tools.

Since I moved away from the land of affordable mental health care, I went a number of years without health insurance that would have made it affordable for me. But eventually I managed to get into a position to go back to therapy, which I did for about a year. This was less about confronting any single dramatic issue, and more of a "checkup and maintenance" type run. Things by and large were running well for me, so I was essentially just getting an outside opinion on how I was doing.

And in the process we confronted some small issues, and I was better for it. When my therapist announced to me that she was moving to another state, I took that as my sign that I was good to stop, and she agreed. The engine was humming along as well as it could without medication.

Because that's the thing—"running good" for me doesn't mean that every day, things are going great. I still struggle with periods of low mood. They aren't triggered by events in my life (my life is pretty damn great, if I'm being honest), but sometimes the chemicals in my brain just get a bit out of whack and my mood slips. Sometimes it's for a few days, sometimes it's for a month.

That's life, and that's ok. I weighed my choices, and I decided that I'm at a point in my life where it isn't bad enough to need medication, and my therapist agreed. But you know what? If it gets to the point where it is dramatically affecting my life, well, then buckle up, buttercup, because I will get the next tool I need to keep this mental house of cards in one piece.

Fire Cut with Smoke: Being a Creative with Depression

I'm better now, but even with all the tools in the world, sometimes depression is just going to win out, hopefully only for a brief period. During one such period for me (which was thankfully only a few months long), I wrote would become this chapter as a blog post on my website. I wrangled with including it. I mean, I just gave you a chapter all about my mental health history—why include one yet another downer interlude? I don't want to beat a dead horse . . . even if that horse deserves it.

But in the end I opted to include it, because I really want to drive home how important transparency is for me and how much I want to normalize conversations like this. Chronologically, this chapter was written well after most of the last one, but still a couple years back. Also, I'm better now, just to be clear. But here we go, my mental state during the darkest days of Covid:

I've been listening to the song "Pale Ghosts" by Panopticon quite a bit of late. I'm listening to it as I write this, in fact. It's a bleak, heavy song but one tinged with hopeful notes. I haven't a clue what the lyrics are—it's a metal song filled with growling vocals—but there is an undercurrent in it that just sort of calls to me. It's been a good metaphor for how I feel as a creative these days.

Some days the words just flow, spilling onto the page in a torrent, and I move down my checklist of tasks one after the other with a feeling of intense satisfaction. On those days, I am the fire of creativity made manifest. Those are the days where people ask, "How do you write so much?" and I swell a little bit with pride.

But those days grow farther and farther apart here lately. My depression is back like it hasn't been in years. I'm sure the isolation of Covid has a bit to do with it, as does the lack of vacation. My diet certainly isn't helping. But mostly it's just the chemicals in my brain, messing about in the wrong ways. I have absolutely no reason to be unhappy, and every reason to be gloriously joyful (my LadyFriend has been the primary reason for that), but science bows to no man, and sometimes the fire turns to a blanket of smothering smoke.

The ideas never slow for me, though, so I just add them to the list. And as the list grows ever larger, it feeds into the despair that I will never be able to achieve even a fraction of what I want to. I think about my mortality and know that if I died tomorrow, from a creative standpoint, no one would ever care. I have not built a legacy of any sort creatively, and as I age, I continue to worry if I ever will.

I saw *Hamilton* the other day, and when they sang about Hamilton ("Why do you write like you're running out of time?"), it honestly made me tear up a bit. I felt it down deep, because I write like that, when the smoke clears. Because I have to, if I am ever going to make it.

When the depression lays on me thickest, it's almost impossible to start new writing projects, though. It's not a writer's block, it's starting block. If I can muster the willpower to make myself open a blank page, words can flow. It's just I struggle so hard to make myself begin. Take this blog post as a perfect example. It took me about three days to build up the gumption to open up my blog, but now that I have, the words are flowing. But this is just a blog post, nothing like the novels and novellas I want to be writing. If it takes that much just to start a blog, how much willpower does it take to start a novel?

With actual writing, though (not blogs, not Fiverr gigs, not silly little Facebook stories), the stories that matter to me most like my novellas and books, I've become so hard on myself. On the good days when fire is running down my fingers, I can write and write and never look back. When the pallid smoke of depression is heavy, though, everything I write is terrible, trash, not worth the virtual ink it took to put it all down. I hate it, and that hate makes me stop. And once I have stopped, the process of actually starting back has to begin over all again.

So I try to distract myself with other things. My shirts have been a good project for this. I am not a graphic designer, so I have been learning rapidly all manner of new tricks and skills. Every little victory like that feeds into the fire. And that feels good. But then I try to sell them, and nothing happens, that feels . . . terrible. This is not a plea for you to go out and buy a shirt, because honestly the thought of someone going out and buying a shirt out of pity just makes me want to throw up out of angst and self-loathing.

Objectively I know that I am new at this, that the economy is trash, that it's going to take time. But as each day passes without any sales, it's a resounding indictment that my designs are just not good enough. It's an internal accusation that I can easily shrug off when my mind is right. But currently, my mind is not right, and it undoes any positive motivation my learning has imparted.

My books don't sell. My shirts don't sell. My games get downloaded, but don't sell. My blogs post unremarked. I generate content, but currently it seems that not any people want to buy for any reason other than they know me. Which, while I will never stop being thankful for all my wonderful friends who support me,

I refuse to make my "living" off of my friends' charity and pity, even if I could.

Not-depressed me knows that I have been sitting on my best ideas, that they are getting edited, and one day soon those books will be out. That I will hit upon shirts that do sell great. That my games will spread. That one day I will master actually marketing in a real, tangible way outside of setting up at conventions and libraries. That the economy will eventually turn around.

But depressed me says I am just screaming into the void, and no one is listening. And I can't do anything about that right now.

I am tired, so tired. Whenever I am home, I am either asleep or working on shirts these days. Every weekend on my off days, I spend a good chunk of that time writing for Fiverr or trying to make some headway, no matter how small, on a game or story. I try to always be hustling. Because if I don't, I am never going to make it to where I want to be.

But I am tired. I almost always feel like I need a nap, which is likely 50% sleep apnea at work and 50% depression dragging me down. And the more tired I am, the worse I feel, depression-wise.

Thursday, I get to go on vacation for ten days, the first vacation I have had all year. I had been spending time thinking about how much I was going to try and get done during it. That I needed to make the most of my time off. That I wanted to take five days and try and write for eight hours a day each day, to treat it like I would if I was finally able to do this full-time.

But writing this has caused me to realize that I need rest. Ten days of nothing but curling up with good books, video games, and the LadyFriend. To go for long walks to clear my head. To not even think about the hustle. Because the hustle will be there when I come back. But if I don't get my mind right, then I may as well not bother.

One day, Covid will pass. Then I will be able to get back into therapy. And then all my plans that this damn sickness ruined can be dusted off and made new. Eventually things will get back to normal, and the fire will fill my veins once more. I just need to clear my veins of smoke first.

Better days are coming. It's a dark, heavy song right now, but I can hear the haunting optimism of the notes underlying the piece. Better days are coming, and then I can once more begin to write like I'm running out of time, before I actually do.

Fellow Underachiever, You Are Seen!

At ConCarolinas 2023, I went to a panel to support my friend Joe Compton (who is amazing and you should go check out his network on YouTube, GoIndieNow). It was on the films of Kevin Smith, which, while I am a fan, I'm not a *"go to a panel at ten o'clock at night when there are some lonely beers looking longingly at my lips"* kind of fan. But Joe is my brother from another mother, and I wasn't going to dip into that sack of Guinness without him, so to the panel I went.

The moderator, whom I won't name, had an incredibly touching moment talking about *Clerks III*. I don't recall the exact wording, but the gist of their thought was that the movie really hit them, and hit them hard. They talked about how the movie highlighted folks of around our age for whom life hadn't turned out right, and how for the first time, they felt *seen*.

That statement really resonated with me. Not because I've seen the movie and agree (I haven't seen it, because I'm a slacker), but that plaintive feeling that something, somewhere along the pathway of our lives went wrong, and no one of authority seemed to really notice or care—that struck a chord. Because I've spent most of my adult life feeling that way. And if you're reading this, there is a decent chance you have too.

I am right on the cusp between the generations. I'm just a nudge into millennial, missing Gen X by a few years. And I think it was with those at the tail end of Gen X that it began (at least in my anecdotal experience), a problem that fully came to blossom by the time my generation came along. We were the children of the baby boomers, a generation that established the great American promise that if you just worked hard and got a degree, you were guaranteed a good job. A house, a wife, and 2.1 kids would promptly follow, if that's what you were into.

I have this bizarrely vivid memory of being in fifth grade working on a mural and having this clear vision that when I graduated college, I would have a job making $50,000 a year right out the gate. It seemed so reasonable, just a forgone conclusion (I will firmly acknowledge that I have more than a little privilege here). And sure, in fifth grade, you don't have a real clue what that actually means. But nowhere along the way did I see any information that ran counter to that. It was a forgone conclusion: go to college, get a good-paying job. The dollar amount was never really spelled out, because it didn't need to be; it would be enough to get that nice house in the 'burbs, no problem.

But by the time we started coming out of college, that degree had gone from a guaranteed ticket to a good job to more and more being the bare minimum to get *any* sort of job that paid better than minimum wage. There had been a bait and switch. Along the way, the price of our ticket had gone through the roof while, instead of being front-row seats to the economic dream, we were stuck back in the nosebleeds.

I graduated in December of 2006. In 2007, I got a raise at my first post-college job as I was promoted to supervisor. I was making $16.88 an hour, around $35,000 a year pre-tax.

The economy tanked in 2008, and I got laid off.

It wasn't until the year of our lord 2023 that I have come to make more than that $16.88/hour. Now, I'm up to around $49,000 a year pre-tax. (I'm a state employee. Our pay is public information, and honestly I don't mind sharing it with you anyway.)

Was this true for all of us? Of course not. I have a cousin—our class clown, in fact—he's something crazy like an ADA. Hell, he's probably going to be governor before it's all said and done. But the bulk of the people in my life? Especially so many of the bright ones, the folks that you would think would just be killing it at life? Very few of them are living the life that we were once told was coming our way. More and more, the bright ones became the broken ones as we've been dashed on life's rocky shores. And only now that we're a decade or two behind schedule are we even getting hints of fixing the cracks. It's only been in the past few years that any significant number of my friends have become established enough to be able to have kids. Some have begun buying houses.

But most of my friends are childless, and rent instead of own. And there is nothing wrong with that. But I'm guessing, based on my own experience, that they feel in some way like they have failed to achieve what they could have or should have. Because I know I have.

Not to sugarcoat things, but I was a really smart kid—Duke TIP student, full-ride scholarship, Mensa-level test scores (that I was too broke to afford the dues to), the works. I could have done pretty much anything I set my mind to. I got some useless degrees, sure, but any job I've had, I've excelled at. If someone gives me a chance, I pretty much rock it. But there just haven't been a lot of chances thrown my way, and I will certainly own the fact that for a long time I didn't run around chasing a chance at something better.

Partially because I'm probably the least money-focused person I know. But I also didn't have many people in my formative years that I could look to as an example. Everyone in my daily life was struggling. Hell, if it wasn't for the kindness of friends and my parents, there were a couple of times I would have been homeless. But you know what? I'm ok with it all. Really. I've always been an underachiever by most any conventional metric you could use, having only in the past couple of years really gotten back "*on track*" (whatever that means).

Because you know what? We didn't get what we were told was coming our way. But I think all that struggle along the way, it made a lot of us far better people than we would have been otherwise. I know it's true for me. The older I've gotten, the more I've struggled, the more empathic it's made me. I pick up hitchhikers, I give money to panhandlers, I drop money I don't have on folks' GoFundMe campaigns. Because I've been down and out, and it was only because folks rallied around me that I got through it. So, I try to return the favor, and everyone I know is the same way. We're a damn helpful, kind generation.

Some folks have taken the hurt of broken promises and gone down dark paths, becoming hateful. Sure, I've had former friends take all that anger and turn toward hate, railing against whatever scapegoat they've settled on for why their lives didn't turn out "*right*." But by and large, I look around and see so many people who are so damn good.

We didn't achieve the house in the suburbs and the brood of kids. But so many of us, freed from the expectation of what we knew we weren't going to achieve, we instead chased our dreams. It took some of us a long time to find them, but when we did, we chased hard. And you know, we may never get there—I may never become a full-time writer. But that will be ok.

I'm used to things not panning out the way they were "*supposed*" to. Because along the way, I have met so many people just like me. The amazing people who make me sit there and think, "*Man, I don't get why someone isn't giving them a chance, 'cause they could rock the whole damn world.*"

They are my people. The underachievers that, be it from some force internal or external, haven't gotten to where they want to be. But given the choice between being crabs in a bucket or a helping hand, they choose to help out every time. I think about my con family, and how everyone is always struggling to break out and break big but never pauses for even a second when given a chance to help a fellow creative get their chance.

So, yeah . . . I see you. And I hope you see me, and know that I have your back. We'll get there. Or we won't. But either way, we'll be together.

Fellow underachiever, you are loved.

By the Numbers

Ok, all of that more emotional stuff is done with, I promise! I hope I didn't scare you off, but I also really hope that something I said in there helped someone realize they are a little less alone than they think. Either way, this chapter is here to give you the actual numbers I promised you in the intro of this section.

Want to see the up-to-date numbers? Go to my website and click on the Transparency tab, or go to my blog. Every month I recap all my sales and socials—lots of good stuff there. But in case all you ever do is crack open this one book, here they are: my numbers as of May(ish) 2024, a couple of months or so before this book came out.

Total Income:

$2,111.94 – 2020
$2,601.11 – 2021
$3,550.33 – 2022
$10,461.07 – 2023

$4,799.64 – 2024
Grand Total: $23,524.09

Books Sold:

In Person: 588
Online: 3,114
Combined: 3,702
KENP Read: 318,757 (the equivalent of 1,104 books)
E-books given away: 5,268

Total Reviews and Average Rating (Amazon):

Bringing Home the Rain (Book 1): 227/4.5
The Depth of the Water (Book 2): 120/4.7
Feet in the Fire (Book 3): 97/4.7
Praying the Day's Not Poison (Book 4): 74/4.7
Walking the Darkness Down (Book 5): 65/4.8
Calling the Devil Partner (Book 6): 37/4.9
Southern Saudade: 17/4.6

Social Media Numbers:

Facebook Page: 933 (When I started tracking in August 2020: 554)

Facebook Group: 278 (When I started tracking in December 2020: 115)

Instagram: 643 (When I started tracking in August 2020: 320)

YouTube Channel: 110 (When I started tracking in August 2020: 61)

Email List: 384 (When I started tracking in December 2021: 80)

Discord: 37 (When I started tracking in 2023: 37)

Book Launch Data (From My Book Six Launch)

The data from the launches will be formatted like this: Book 6 Data (Book 1, Book 2, Book 3, Book 4, Book 5)

Launch Week Order Numbers:

Day 1: Paid: 238 (43, 14, 181, 142, 500)   Free: 351 (0, 0, 623, 720, 832)

Day 2: Paid: 107 (3, 8, 34, 59, 147)   Free: 71 (0, 0, 96, 158, 258)

Day 3: Paid: 30 (6, 3, 22, 17, 25)   Free: 66 (0, 0, 74, 62, 76)

Day 4: Paid: 5 (2, 2, 7, 8, 27)   Free: 107 (0, 0, 35, 26, 51)

Day 5: Paid: 4 (1, 2, 3, 10, 21)   Free: 1 (0, 0, 4, 6, 3)

Day 6: Paid: 6 (1, 1, 6, 6, 6)   Free: 0 (420, 0, 0, 0)

Day 7: Paid: 6 (0, 0, 2, 9, 4)   Free: 0 (141, 0, 0, 0)

Total Paid: 396 (56, 30, 255, 251, 730)

Total Free: 595 (561, 0, 832, 972, 1,220)

KENP:

Day 1: 4,322 (175, 28, 334, 544, 1,622)

Day 2: 1,672 (10, 116, 592, 559, 1,479)

Day 3: 1,697 (307, 516, 1,341, 1,284, 1,733)

Day 4: 1,010 (0, 383, 1,264, 1,176, 2,137)

Day 5: 1,479 (0, 116, 818, 570, 3,065)

Day 6: 491 (53, 141, 2,015, 258, 2,807)

Day 7: 1,341 (265, 79, 1,428, 1,287, 2,216)

Totals: 12,012 (810, 1,379, 7,792, 5,678, 15,059)

Day of Week/Month for Day One of the Launch:

Book 1: Sunday/August

Book 2: Saturday/November

Book 3: Wednesday/January

Book 4: Tuesday/August

Book 5: Wednesday/March

Book 6: Wednesday/July–August

Sale Price Strategy

Book 1: Set to free five days after launch.

Book 2: Nothing.

Book 3: Free/.99

Book 4: Free/.99/.99

Book 5: Free/.99/.99/1.99/3.99

Book 6: Free/.99/.99/1.99/1.99/3.99

Behind the Scenes for a Week in the Life of Bob the Author

Putting out books is the main thrust of what I do, obviously. There are a lot of things that go into that, which I cover on my blog or on social media. For this chapter, though, I thought I would give you an idea of some of the things I end up doing that further the cause but don't get much press, as it were, to give you some insight into what all it might entail to do what I do.

Why? Not because I think you need to be doing all these things as well, but because I want to show you what things CAN look like. To get your mind churning, and thinking outside the box. Remember the core message: you have to be creative, and use that creativity to get noticed.

So, here it is, the list of things I did in the week after coming back from Atlanta Comic Con 2024:

1. Emailed an employee at Alabama Comic Con,

following up on plans to try and coordinate a track for table swap.

2. Reached out to a local writing workshop to discuss me possibly presenting (I was denied).

3. Called Ben to discuss CONjuration table space and about a room at ASPC. One of about a half dozen small conversations with Ben, actually (we stay plottin'!).

4. Applied to CONjuration and started thinking about what panels I want to submit.

5. Talked to a small con that's just starting this year, offering myself as a resource about their vendor hall practices (which, from what I saw, were outside the norm from any con I've ever attended).

6. Messaged a track director who had expressed to me that they wanted to conduct more interviews at area conventions, letting them know about a different con I saw that had an application specifically for that.

7. Talked to one of my cohosts about the timeline of when we will be kicking Books, Beards, Booze back up. Recruited a replacement cohost for the other cohost spot, who had to step away due to life.

8. An author reached out to me asking to connect me with an author friend of theirs who is thinking of starting a podcast. So, I sent a follow-up email to said author, and we started emailing back and forth.

9. Made plans to go visit a location to see if it would be a suitable spot to host an author event I'm planning.

10. Tried to reach out to an author whose publicist has now sent me two books of theirs (for no reason that I can really divine), trying to let them know their publicist may be wasting their money. They never responded, so now I have two books on Mexican cheese.

11. Worked on my presentations for the Atlanta Self-Publishing Conference, the Alabama Writing Workshop, and the Atlanta Writing Workshop. Got my "Organic Marketing for Authors" PowerPoint mostly made.

12. Wrote three blog posts, including the original blog post that contained all this information.

13. Ordered new stickers to sell, as I'm getting low in some of my categories.

14. Ordered bags in two types, one for books and one for stickers.

15. Email four local universities and the local magnet high school about guest speaking. Got zero responses.

16. Sent my new author photos to my publisher.

17. Touched base with my audiobook narrator to nail down some marketing stuff to start making some announcements in the coming week.

18. Reached out to a screenwriter I'm working with to follow up on a project.

19. Saw that there was an author Q&A going on at my local library, so I reached out to see if I could take part as an author (got accepted, and it was too much fun!).

20. Applied to a small con in Birmingham that is just starting back up as a vendor using their application. I then sent a follow-up email pitching myself as a guest/panelist with a link to my convention resume.

So, yeah, it was a lot of little things. None of them took more than a few minutes usually, and any one of them could have, in some small way, led to the next big jump forward in my career. You never know! For example, I can share that from that list of items, here are a few things that came of them:

1. At that library event, I met an author I had

been wanting to meet for a while, and we got to network a bit. She runs an event I will be taking part in next year.

2. Books, Beards, Booze is coming back in a big way. We recruited our new cohost (Ben Meeks, remember him?) and got our first five episodes recorded.

3. I still have one book about Mexican cheese. I ended up giving one to Ben.

4. I got to mentor, in a small way, a couple of newer authors I met at the library event in follow-up emails post-event.

The Calculus of Trad Publishing vs. Self-Publishing Capitol of Nightmares

So, in case you missed it, Falstaff Books—through their horror imprint, Falstaff Dread—will be publishing my horror novel, *Capitol of Nightmares*. If you're holding this sometime in 2025, there's a decent chance it's already out, and you should go buy it! No, really, this book will still be here when you get back. Go snag it, it's great.

Anyway, I wanted to explain why I made the choice to go that route instead of self-publishing it. "But Bob, I've attended your 'how to get published' workshop in the past, and you typically advise that if given the choice between traditional publishing with a small press or self-publishing, you would almost always choose to self-pub!" This is true, and I absolutely stand by that statement and mindset, especially for newer authors. The fact of the matter is this:

1. You probably don't have the knowledge to tell a good small press from a bad one early on (I certainly didn't).

2. Most small presses, even if they are reputable, don't bring enough to the table to justify what you have to give up.

All that said, there are absolutely exceptions to every rule. Small press can mean "we put out a couple of small anthologies a year," or it can mean "we put out about a hundred novels a year" and all points in between/around. If you want to publish a short story, then sure, go small press with reckless abandon (you're not gonna make any money anyway, let's be real). But for something like a novel, you need to do your research.

1. What is their social media presence like? If it's only a couple hundred people, then what are they bringing to the table marketing-wise?

2. Do they do events that are going to get your books in front of people? Or do they only focus on online sales?

3. What do authors who have worked with them have to say? Are they happy?

4. What's the vibe? Do they seem like good people? Do the authors they publish seem like

good people?

I was absolutely prepared to self-publish *Capitol of Nightmares*. In fact, the only reason I hadn't was that it's decently long (102,000 words) and I just wasn't in the mood to pay to have it edited. That was going to be a decent chunk of change, and I had other books with a higher editing priority. It had been sitting there just waiting on me to email it to Cleo (my editor), basically, but then Falstaff asked me to submit.

Based on the questions you need to ask that I listed out above, I thought it out:

1. They have a larger social media presence than me, and they are not afraid to experiment with things like TikTok.

2. They do events ALL THE TIME. My books will be on a table in front of folks at a bunch of events I can't get to myself.

3. I'm friends with a lot of their authors, and no one has shit-talked them to me. The biggest complaint I've heard is "I wish my book was out already," which, yeah, that's gonna be literally every press of any size's biggest complaint, lol. Publishing books is slow work. Falstaff is typically faster than bigger presses, but they can never be as fast as self-pub. Just the way things are.

4. Vibe check: I have yet to meet anyone Falstaff-related who's sketchy (well, John's a redneck, but what can ya do?). And a couple of folks who I intensely, intensely respect are put out by them (including the chief editor for Falstaff Dread, Rachel Brune).

Also, Falstaff is very well connected with the Southern convention circuit. Most of the fan-run cons have some sort of presence from someone at Falstaff; it's a very-known element within those circles.

It's not all sunshine and roses, however. The odds are that I would have made more money in direct dollars by self-publishing it. That's just the nature of the beast. That wouldn't be true for everyone who sells through them, but I hustle enough on my own that between the in-person events I do and my online promoting, I would sell enough to make more that way. So, why do it then? Why opt to (probably) make less money?

For me, it's all about the intangibles. I'm gambling that whatever I give up in direct dollars from sales, I will make back in intangible benefits.

1. Falstaff is well-known in the types of conventions I like to take part in. Being associated with them will make it easier for me to become a guest at these conventions, which gives me more selling opportunities as well as more chances to panel. Paneling is a fantastic way to grow my brand, and I am always looking to do

more.

2. I will be traditionally published. (Yes, techni-
cally I already am, but that was a pretty bad
experience and I rarely mention it, remember?
Those books are under a different name for a
reason.) Should that matter? In a perfect world,
no. But there's no two ways about it: There will
always be a group of people for whom you are
simply not credible as an author if all you do is
self-pub. Thankfully, that's an ever-decreasing
number, but it's still a factor. Being traditionally published makes my self-published works
more credible in their eyes.

3. It makes me more attractive to the folks who
run workshops and offer speaking opportunities. I have really been trying to amp this up
over the past year, and by being both traditionally published *and* self-published, it could open
more doors for me.

Let's use some totally bogus numbers just to make
a point. If I self-published it, let's say I would make
$1,000 off it a year. And let's say by Falstaff putting
it out, I make $300. That's a loss of $700 bucks a
year—not great. But let's say that because I am now
trad published through Falstaff, I . . .

1. Get into JordanCon as a guest next year, get to
sell my books (my white whale of conventions),

and make a profit of $400. (A reasonable number—I just cleared $550 at my last event.)

2. Get to do a workshop with the AWP that nets me a $250 speaking fee.

3. Get onto more panels at Dragon Con, which gets me in front of a bunch of folks who I would have never run into otherwise who end up buying some of my books to the tune of $100.

Boom, I've made more money than I would have by self-publishing, by fifty bucks. Now, of course, all these numbers are bullshit and made-up, but you can see how it *could* play out.

But I know me and how I operate, and I think I'm right about this. But also—and this doesn't factor into anything business related—for me, this is sorta coming full circle. I went self-pub on the recommendation of John G. Hartness during a mentor session at Dragon Con. In that talk, he broached this topic in a general sense, starting my brain down this thought process, and now he's publishing me. It just feels . . . right.

In the immortal words of Bear Bryant, when asked why he returned to Alabama in 1958 to coach the Crimson Tide:

"Momma called. And when Momma calls, you just have to come runnin'."

Section Four: Specific Guides!

In this section, I'm taking a few guides I've written up on my blog and reworking them a bit here to help get you started. If you've already been checking me out on my website, then this may be old hat for you. If not, though, I have some neat guides here to help jump-start your career as a creative!

Six Easy Steps to Getting Started as a Business

"I Have No Money and I Must Sell": A Six-Week Guide to Super Basic Infrastructure as a Creative

You are a creative, and you're just starting out. You have no money, but you need to start getting the word out there and maybe start getting some sales. Also, you're broke, so your time is usually spent, you know, surviving. So, here it is: a six-week guide to getting set up as a creative. Each week, you have one fairly simple task to complete to get you there. If you are a real go-getter, you could do one a day, but hey, life is life—if you do one a week, you'll be in good shape.

- **Week One: Set Up Your Linktree**

- You don't have a website yet, so this is going to be the stand-in for now. It costs nothing, and you control what links go on it. When you pick your name for it, try to make it something that you can also use for your social media account names. Smart money says you should check to see if they are free on the sites you plan to use (and maybe go ahead and lock those in). Maybe even see if the domain name is available.

- **Week Two: Set Up Your Primary Social Media Account**

- Pick whatever form of social media you're most comfortable with: Instagram, Facebook, Twitter, TikTok, whatever. Set up your account on there, and start using it regularly. Starting out, it may be hard, but here's my advice: Do a series of introductory posts (five or six) the day you set it up. Now, commit to at least one post a week on there. Maybe set a reminder in your phone. Make it visual, either a picture or video, and put your Linktree as a link in the bio. Put a link to this social media account in the Linktree as well.

- **Week Three: Set Up Your Secondary Social Media Account**

- Pick the form of social media you're *next* most comfortable with. This is your backup platform in case you have to stop using the other one, life changes, or who knows what else. Start using it in the same manner as the above. Two accounts is plenty to start with. If you're thinking, "Man, how on earth am I going to keep up with two social media accounts?" well . . . this may not be the life path for you. Spoiler: You will probably end up spending as much time marketing/networking as you spend creating, unless you blow up to the point you can afford to pay someone to do it for you. Again, put a link to your Linktree in the bio. Put a link to this account in the Linktree.

- **Week Four: Set Up Your Newsletter**

- I have an in-depth guide in the next chapter, but in short, find a free service like MailerLite and set up an account. Use their service to generate a free landing page, and then put a link to it in your Linktree. Once you have some subscribers (it may take some time—you're just starting out, that's ok), send your first newsletter. Send another one a month after that. Repeat monthly until death or retirement.

- **Week Five: Order a Business Card**

- This is going to cost you, but it won't cost a lot if you look around. Price shop, look for promo codes, etc. You need to order five hundred one-sided business cards. Put your name and your business name on it, and if you have a website, include that link as well. Now go to your Linktree and find the Share button.

Click that, then click the link to get a QR code for your Linktree. Download it and add it to your card. This is going to be how you market yourself in person, and it will help you with networking. Don't put your email or phone number on there. If someone needs to have it (like that publisher you ran into who asked you to send them a draft of your book), then you can write it for them on the back of the card. But also make sure you get their info, because honestly, it's more likely that you'll follow up with them than vice versa.

- **Week Six: Set Up a PayPal/Square**

- I'm old-school—I still use PayPal fairly often. I link it to my business bank account and run a lot of my business money through it from more niche sites that use it. But I also use Square, especially for in-person sales. If you have a phone with an audio jack or lightning cable jack, you can get them to send you a free magstripe reader that will allow you to swipe credit cards using your phone. Have that, along with a handful of change, and you are set to start making in-person sales! For more about doing your first in-person event, I have a guide for you coming up two chapters from now.

More Complex/Costly Next Steps:

This list is not exhaustive; it's just a few things to get you thinking. You'll need to do some of these things, for sure. Others, not as much. And there a billion more things not listed here! These are just some of the high notes:

1. You need a website. Yes, there are free options, but folks are URL snobs. It's sad, but true. If they see *authorname.wixsite.blah*, they're gonna think, "They don't take this seriously, so why should I check out their product? They probably don't take that seriously, either." So, go for a domain and website that gets you to authorname.com or the like. Typically you can pay for a year at a time, or in three-year chunks. Do what you can afford.

2. You need a business license and such. This is way more complicated than I can explain. If you get gummed up, look for your local Small Business Administration office. They will help you out, for free.

3. You may want to add more social media accounts to your repertoire. Remember: It's better to not have a social media account than to have one that you don't update. This can include things like Goodreads if you're an author.

4. You can look into sites like TeePublic and Redbubble if you're an artist. They are online

print-on-demand stores, which will enable you to get sales without having to carry any inventory/pay up front. You won't make as much profit as with other ways, but the other ways cost money and require you to carry inventory that may or may not sell.

5. The flip side of this for authors is a site like Amazon (using KDP) or Ingram Spark. They are also print-on-demand, so you don't have to carry inventory, and you can make online sales. Then, whenever you plan to sell at live events, you can usually order books at cost plus shipping ahead of time to be your inventory.

6. You can look into setting up an account on Fiverr or the like to freelance and build up funds to pay for more expensive things, like websites and editing.

A Quick Guide to Newsletters

Are you an author? Then you need a newsletter. Go set one up.

That should be the end of this post, but I suppose I should address some common issues I've seen crop up! There has been a bizarre amount of pushback on this snippet of advice lately from some quarters, which is why I'm going to lay it out for you. So, here's the how and why of newsletters from a guy who is ok at them.

Why a Newsletter?

I have around 715 subscribers to my newsletter. I average right around a 40% open rate on it, which means a few hundred folks get my email and actively click on it to check it out. Have you ever had a social media post that had even close to that sort of engagement? Probably not, unless you were lucky enough to have something go really viral. Here are some other points:

1. There's no algorithm blocking it from being seen by some of your followers.

2. You have total control of your own newslet-

ter, unlike social media, which can change the
rules at any point.

3. You can take it with you. If my host, MailerLite,
   goes to close down, all I have to do is click a
   button to export my mailing list, and boom, I
   have it and can upload it anywhere else I so
   choose. I used to be on Mailchimp before I
   swapped; I just exported my list and loaded it
   into MailerLite. Boom. Easy.

4. The folks who signed up did so willingly. They
   have let you know that yes, they want to hear
   from you! The kind of folks who do that tend
   to be booklovers, and they want to know more
   about your books.

5. I don't care that "Gen Z doesn't like email"
   or that "millennials hate newsletters." Maybe
   some do. And you know what? Those who do
   actually hate them can find me in other places!
   I'm on social media too—it's not a zero-sum
   game. But guess what: *no group is a monolith.*
   You're not trying to target *Gen Z*, you're trying to target *readers*. And tons of readers love
   newsletters.

6. To have a successful social media presence, you
   have to be pretty active. We're talking multiple
   posts a week, if not more. To have a success-

ful newsletter, though? One email a month. If you're the type who can generate the content, once a week at most (*glares at Brian Keene, the successful bastard*).

Ok, I'm Sold. How Do I Set One Up? How Do I Grow It?

Setting it up is easy peasy. Growing it will be a slog. Here is your rough order of actions:

1. Find a newsletter host like Mailchimp, Mailer-Lite, etc. Find one that's free since you're just starting out. There are a lot of options that start out free and only charge once you get to the point where you have, like, two to five thousand subscribers. It'll probably be a long time before you have to worry about hitting that number, and when you do, it will likely be worth it to start paying. Just look around first and see if there's maybe a better spot elsewhere if you do have to pay. Ask your author friends who they use.

2. Sign up.

3. The site will generate a landing page where folks can sign up online.

4. Add a link to this landing page to your Linktree (which is also free).

5. Make sure your social media accounts have a link to your Linktree in the bio.

6. Most of the time, the site will have an option to give you the code to embed a sign-up form right on your website. Do that! If you can't embed it, then have a link there that takes them to your landing page.

7. Long-term, consider setting up some sort of freebie like a short story or novella that, when they sign up, folks will receive in their email.

8. Get a clipboard and print off some sheets where folks can sign up by hand. Set it on your table at every event you're a part of. I would say I get between five and twenty-five new emails per event, depending on length.

9. You can set up newsletter swaps with other authors! Find authors who write stuff similar to you, and swap links in each other's emails.

10. Sign up to take part in email builders. Courtney Cannon runs some that I've used in the past that worked well for me.

But I'm Just Starting Out/I'm Not That Interesting!

The most common question I hear is, "What do you put in a newsletter when you might not even have a book out yet?" Here are my thoughts:

- For now, just focus on doing one newsletter a month. (And that may never change for you. We can't all be Brian Keene.)

- Here are book-related topics you can include:

1. A snippet from something you wrote this month.

2. What events you're going to be a part of.

3. A book review of a book similar to what you write.

4. The status of how much you've written.

5. Where you're at in the publishing process.

6. Some art you made/had commissioned for your characters.

- The folks who sign up for newsletters, they typically want more than just book news—they want to learn more about the person behind the books. So, here are examples of things I've done or seen people include in their newsletters:

1. I like Legos, so I've started recreating little

scenes from my books with them. I will occasionally put a picture of a scene at the very end of my newsletter.

2. People love cats. It's common for authors to include pet pictures.

3. One author puts a raunchy meme at the end (they write erotica).

4. I love board games. Sometimes I put board game-related content in there.

5. Sometimes I'll link to a blog post I wrote that I was proud of.

6. It's not uncommon for me to put a link to a shirt design of mine, or maybe to my indie RPGs I sell.

Here's a rough template you can try:
Nonnegotiable:

- **Picture** – Maybe it's you, your book, you doing a book-related thing, a promo image, etc.

- **Text Block** – News related to your book, such as appearances, excerpts, publishing news, sales, etc.

Optional:

- **Another Picture** – Include a picture related to

something personal. A hobby of yours, a book you just read, etc.

- **Text Block** – Explain the above picture.

- **Another Picture** – Include a picture related to the newsletter swap if you're doing one that month.

- **Text Block** – Explain the above picture and include a link about the author/book you're newsletter swapping with.

- **Another Picture** – Include a picture related to something fun. This is probably going to be a picture of your pets, but it can really be whatever note you want to end on.

- **Text Block** – Explain the above picture.

Want to see one in action and have an example to steal ideas from? Sign up for mine! Just go to my website, talesbybob.com!

A Guide to Selling at Your First In-Person Event!

Are you a creative thinking about doing your first in-person event to sell your works? Then this little guide is for you! Keep in mind I am an author, so this won't be a one-to-one guide if you're an artist, musician, etc., but by and large the advice should hold true for you as well. So, let's dive in!

Where's the Party?

Events are all over the place, literally. You should, as a creative, already be going to events (creatives support other creatives!), so that should be the first place you start. Go to the events you usually go to, and while you're there, speak with vendors/organizers to find out how to get involved. **Just ask!** I promise no one is going to bite (unless it's a zombie fest, maybe).

But maybe you live in bumfuck nowhere, and there are no good events around that fit what you do. Are you on Facebook? There are usually regional event groups where folks post calls for vendors. You can search on Facebook for events by your area and see what folks have posted on there. You can also look for sites like southernfan.com, which is a site that does nothing but post fandom events across the Southeastern US.

Lastly, ask your online creative friends. Don't have any? Go check out some folks who are doing what you do, or something similar, in your area. You can reach out and **ask them**, or if you aren't comfortable with that, just watch their socials to see what events they announce they're going to be at. Let that be your guide.

Pre-Gaming!

Ok, so let's say you've found an event you would like to be a part of. Here's what you will need to do, in a rough order:

1. Make sure you're going to be able to actually have inventory by the show date. Author? Make sure you've ordered your books/have them on hand. Artist? Get to painting/ordering prints. There is no point in this if you show up with nothing to sell. Make sure it can arrive/be crafted in time for the show!

2. Keep in mind what sort of price points you have on your items. For your first event, it's probably best to keep it simple. But long-term, you want to have your main product, then a very cheap product, and then a more expensive

product. In my case I have my books—which are $15/$35 each—then stickers that I sell for a buck, and then a book bundle that's $100. Some folks want to support you but maybe don't have the money to buy your main product—that's what the cheap thing is for. Then some folks are gonna LOVE what you do and will want to spend a ton. Have an option for that as well! In the near future, I'm planning to have a super fancy collector edition of my books for those superfans.

3. Order business cards if you don't have them. My recommendation is a simple card with your name, business name, and website, then put a QR code that connects to your Linktree. Don't have one of those? Get one. (It's free, geez! How many times are you going to make me say it?) Look for sites that are offering promo codes where you can get, like, five hundred cards for fifteen bucks.

4. Figure out how you're going to get paid. Cash is great, but a lot of folks don't carry it. I recommend that you look into Square and use that. You'll need to order one of their card swipe devices from them. This will be connected to your bank account, which . . . man, we're getting in the weeds here, but you have a business, right? With its own bank account? Just for your

business? That's a different book, but yeah.

5. Apply to the show! You may get in. You may not. Some shows will ask you for a picture of your setup. If this is your first event, then you may need to get it all out and set it up in your yard/living room and take a picture. Some shows will want links to your socials or website. If you don't have those, well, you may want to consider getting those set up. There will also likely be a table cost.

6. Figure out if this event is providing a table/chairs. If so, you're good! If not, you need a table. Long-term, you're gonna need a table regardless, but I get it—money may be tight. Once you can, I recommend getting a folding six-foot table and a nice tablecloth. I use a plain black one that's fitted, but that's just me. Do whatever makes sense for your branding. For example, I used to use a black-and-white one that had pattern of a skull in a top hat. I eventually decided it was a little busy, but you get the idea.

7. Is this event indoors or outdoors? If it's outdoors, what are you going to do if it rains? Are you like me and sunburn at the drop of a hat? What are you going to do for shade? If you have the money, get a 10x10 pop-up pavilion. If you

hunt around, you can get one for about $100 sometimes. An 8x8 is also a valid option if you are on a budget. They are usually noticeably cheaper.

8. Get a clipboard and print off a few sheets for an email list sign-up. Don't have an email list yet? MailerLite is free (until your list reaches a certain size), so use that. You can always transfer to a better fit later if needed.

9. Make a price sheet for your items. My recommendation is going to Walmart or the like and buying a cheap freestanding picture frame to put it in.

10. Figure out how you're going to display your stuff. Books? You need a book stand. Art? You need a stand, and maybe a box folks can look through or a binder for your prints. Go to places like Michaels and look to see if they're running a sale on what you need, or maybe they have something on clearance. Maybe you have something around your house you can use! Be creative.

11. Set up your table ahead of time, at least once, and see how it looks. Maybe ask some friends their opinions.

12. Decide how you're going to get all the stuff

from your home to the venue. I use a fancy rolling toolbox thingy now, but when I started, I used two totes: one held inventory, one held the table/infrastructure stuff. I loaded them into a wheeled cart and it was heavy as fuck, because I chose poorly by being an author and books are heavy. But it worked.

13. Are you going to be going solo? Can you bring a friend/spouse? Can you share a table? Consider these things. Think about how you're going to handle going to the bathroom if you're there alone. Where will you put your money?

14. At these events, food is often pricey. Can you bring snacks? Drinks? If so, how are you going to do that? Think it through.

15. Load your vehicle the day before so you can make sure everything fits. Maybe gas up ahead of time, go get change if you need it. Think happy thoughts!

Party Time!

It's the day of. It's go time! Here's what you need to do/consider:

1. See what time you're allowed to start setting up and get there at least a few minutes before then. This is your first event ever—you NEED

to get there as early as you can, because you don't know how long it's going to take you to get set up. If you get done way early, good! Use that time to either get your head right, or wander around checking out other vendors/networking a little.

2. You're set up. Now, make sure the method by which you're going to take card payments is set up. I almost always forget to open my Square app until that first sale of the morning. Don't be like me.

3. You can sit there behind your table and not engage with anyone unless they engage with you first. If that's what you have to do, no harm, no foul. I get it. You're new at this, and you may be uncomfortable. I challenge you, however, to *not* do this. Stand up, and at least look at each person walking by and smile a little. Give off a welcoming energy! If you're comfortable with it, engage with folks passing by. Give (non-creepy) compliments. I would avoid complimenting anything physical about their person (again, don't be creepy), but saying things like "Good morning" or "I love your Zelda cosplay!" or "Nice Fallout shirt!" aren't creepy. If they look like they're a reader, I may hit them with a "Do you like to read?" or "What do you like to read?" Get them to notice you. So

many folks will just walk right by and not look, but if you engage, they will at least glance your way, and then maybe they'll stop.

4. Don't be afraid to tweak your setup on the fly. Realize that your price sheet isn't in a good spot? Move it. See that the flow of traffic is the opposite of what you expected? Reorient that display if you need to.

5. I keep a business card or note card set to the side during each event. On this card, I write down any ideas I have for how to improve my setup that I can't execute at that moment. I also write down contact info from networking, ideas unrelated to vending, etc. Write these things down! You have too much going on to try and remember this stuff when the event is over.

6. Stay off your phone as much as possible. Make it look like you are present and want to be there! Having your head down in your phone all the time gives the opposite impression.

7. I know a number of artists (especially fiber artists) who use this time to make more products. They'll sit at their table and crochet away as they sell. This is a good use of time, and shows folks that *yes, I really did make this*. Just

make sure you make a point of looking up frequently and looking inviting.

8. Folks may have a ton of questions. That's not a bad thing! Someone standing at your table talking to you makes it more likely that someone else will stop and check out your stuff too. People's brains are just wired that way.

9. Try to make friends with similar creatives and pick their brains. Ask them what their next event is going to be. Maybe see if there's someone who might want to share a table with you at your next event. Ask them where they get their prints; maybe it's cheaper/better quality than where yours came from?

10. Be a good neighbor. Introduce yourself to the folks on either side of you, maybe offer to watch their stuff if they need to go to the bathroom—that sort of thing.

11. I really can't emphasize this enough: Money is, of course, the main goal of these sorts of events, but a very, *very* close number two is networking. There are lots of opportunities out there waiting for you to network your way into them.

12. HAVE FUN! Really, this stuff can be a lot of fun. I love it, and I hope you will too.

The Hangover!

The show is over, and you are hopefully back at home with a lot less product and a lot more money! Here's what you need to do now:

1. Check your inventory. Do you need to reorder?

2. Send follow-up emails/messages to folks you networked with. Make sure you do this sooner rather than later, as folks may forget you if enough time goes by. Strike while their memory is fresh!

3. That list you made of ideas for your booth? Get it out and start making those changes.

4. Add the emails you gathered into your email list.

5. Take the excess cash to the bank, strip club, etc. (Just make sure you leave enough for change in your cash box/bag.)

6. Start planning that next event!

How I Get Into Conventions

I've gotten asked a couple of times lately how I get into the conventions I get into. So, I thought it might be helpful to have a chapter about it. Keep in mind, the short answer is: be a nice person and **just ask**. But let's see how I turned noes into yeses!

Question one is usually, "How do you find conventions to be in?" At this point, it's usually word of mouth. Authors are always chatting, and we give recommendations for cons we like, ones we sell well at, who to talk to, etc. But to supplement that, I also use websites like southernfan.com since I'm based in the American South.

Also, let's be clear, you can "do" cons without being an official guest. If you're an expert in a Thing but not established enough to be let in as an official guest, you can always reach out and ask to help out on a panel. Many is the con I have attended and volunteered to help fill a seat if they had an opening; I have done this to success at cons ranging from Multiverse to Dragon Con at this point. Just whatever you do, do *not* show up to the panel you want to be on and ask to be let on! Go well in advance, preferably a day or two in the event of multiday cons, or if you can email the week before, see if you can speak to the track/programming director and just let them know you're available and why you would be an asset. Then cross your fingers and hope for a little pity. #goteamweasel

With that out of the way, I'm going to go down the list of the larger conventions I have taken/want to take part in. This is not all of them, by any stretch, so I'll do a sort of blanket "here's what I do for small conventions" entry as well.

- **Multiverse**: As I got more plugged into the author scene, numerous folks told me I needed to be at Multiverse. Before attending, I applied to be a guest. I was not accepted, but enough folks kept singing its praises that I went as an attendee. It was amazing! So, I applied for the next year. In the interim, I got to meet the con chairs at ConCarolinas and established a bromance with the Play Track director. I also had grown my friendship with the woman who's now the programing director (though I didn't realize it at the time, haha). So by that point, all parties concerned had seen me panel and vend at other cons and knew I could show up and not embarrass myself too badly. I've now been a repeat guest.

- **Dragon Con**: 2024 was my first year as an

Attending Professional, which is not quite a full-blown guest, but it means I'm on the list for panels and in the program! But before all that, I networked my way into a number of panels over the years, as well as vending, all by asking. This is also where I've made the most connections that have led directly to guesting at other cons/events.

- **ConCarolinas**: Heard about this one from the Falstaff crew. Nancy Knight also told me to go and apply, and when she says to do something, I do it. John G. Hartness knows me and knows what I'm about, so I was accepted on my first attempt. I've been a guest repeatedly and got to panel alongside the likes of Matt Dinniman (*Dungeon Crawler Carl*) and Kevin J. Anderson (*Dune, Star Wars*, etc.).

- **CONjuration**: I don't remember how I heard about this one. Maybe through Ben Meeks? We both applied, and in our applications we basically explained that they could get us two for one if they wanted. I don't know if that's why they let us in, but it certainly didn't hurt. We now do it every year. I did eleven panels there last year—my record thus far!

- **Chattacon**: I found this one on Southern Fandom and, while looking, happened to see Hartness was guest of honor. So I applied, and I got my friend Alex Nader to apply as well. We both got accepted into the author alley as a package deal.

- **JordanCon**: I *really* want to be in this one. I've applied three times now, I believe? I know at least twice before. Each time, I've been denied. But since the last time, I have buffed up my credentials a bit and met more people who have been involved with it, who were able to vouch for me if asked. So while I was not accepted as a guest this most recent go-around, I did get to do five panels.

- **Small Conventions:** Many smaller cons don't have much in the way of formal application processes for guests. Many don't have established tracks, instead having panel rooms that cover a wide array of topics. When this is the case, I just email them, explain who I am, include a list of cons/panels I have done, and offer to run a panel or two for them. I always make a point of suggesting a topic I can do solo if needed, but I make it clear I can/will accept guests on it or (if I can) offer to help populate the panel. I have, to date, never been turned down. This is how I built my resume early on, and I think this went a long way to establishing the credentials that gave the bigger cons more confidence in bringing me in on as a guest.

Guide to Useful Software for Creatives

One perk of self-publishing is that you have total control.

One downside of self-publishing is that you have total control.

This means that for good or ill, if something has to get done, it's on you to do it, which means either paying someone or learning how to do it yourself. And while there are a few tasks that I feel you should always be ready to pony up some cash for (looking at you, editing), almost everything else, you can learn to do yourself. It just takes time and a little bit of technical competency.

I almost always hate having to pay someone to do anything software related, because I know that if I just had the software and the time, I could teach myself how to do it. Every dollar I save on production costs is money that can be spent on editing the next book, buying some merch, or ordering more copies of books to sell. One common theme you will see across all (but one) of these is that none of them are software that require a monthly fee. For each of them, you buy it once, and you own it. That's why you won't see programs like Adobe (get fucked) or Word on this list.

So, here is my list of the software I've learned to use to do . . . well, whatever I need to do. I'm listing them in the order in which I started using them regularly enough to say I'm at least somewhat proficient with them:

- **Google Drive – Docs/Sheets/Slides/Forms**

- I use this in place of the Microsoft Office suite of products. As an added bonus, it's hosted in the cloud, so wherever I am, I can access it. Whether I'm working on my laptop, my phone, a desktop at a friend's, or whatever, I can pick back up and write anywhere in the world, as well as track information in sheets like my monthly recaps. This is free software.

- **GoDaddy – Website Hosting/Builder**

- Obviously, I pay a recurring fee for this. This isn't really a bit of software; I included it here just to show that this is what I do to build my websites. They provide a website builder as part of the fee, and this means I can make changes on my own as many times as I want without having to go through a webmaster/web designer.

- Honestly, if you plan to have more than one website (like me), I do not recommend GoDaddy. But if you have plans for only one site, it's great! Slightly pricey, but I think it's worth the expense. Check it out.

- **Audacity – Audio Editing/Podcasts**

- Audacity is an open-source audio editing software. Whenever I record a podcast, I take the MP3 file and drop it into Audacity to adjust the overall volume levels, add in the intro and outro, that sort of thing. You can also use Audacity to make recordings, and if you're doing a solo podcast, it's actually great for that. It just runs into some issues, I've found, when you try to use multiple microphones and the like. That may have changed over time, but I've already moved on. This is free software.

- **Affinity Designer – Vector Editing/Marketing/Covers**

- Affinity Designer is a direct competitor to Adobe Illustrator. And you know what? You don't have to pay each month to use it! I use it to make all of my promo images and my book covers. It's a really powerful tool, and honestly I only use a fraction of its capabilities (because

I haven't as yet had to use them). There are tooooons of YouTube videos that will teach you all manner of niche use cases. I got this (and the two companion products, Publisher and Photo) for $25 each during Covid. When they released the second edition of it, I was able to get them all for $25 each again.

- **OBS – Open Broadcasting Software/Recording Podcasts**

- Remember how I said I moved on from Audacity for recording? I used Pro Tools for a bit, then shifted to Zoom. But Pro Tools was expensive (I was using a free version that I refused to upgrade), and Zoom had a monthly fee to record longer than forty-five minutes, which, most of the time, I am. So, I finally took the plunge of learning OBS . . . which was actually a lot easier than when I tried to do so years ago. You can use it for livestreaming, recording livestreams, recording, pretty much anything. This is how I record things like Books, Beards, Booze and my workshops. This is free software.

- **Affinity Publisher – More Complex Book Layouts/Zines**

- I've had Affinity Publisher as long as I've had Designer, but I only recently (2024) started actively using it. It's book layout software, and I will be honest, it's a bit more complicated than I would like for just laying out a normal book. Powerful, but that power comes at a cost, and that's total ease of use. But I am loving it for zine layouts! Zines are more complex to design, so they really need that power.

- **Atticus – Book Layouts**

- Atticus, however, is about as intuitive as you could ever want when it comes to book layouts. This is what I'm using for all my book layouts now. If you like how the insides of this book looks, you can thank Atticus for that. If you hate it, blame me—I probably fucked it up. Upload your edited file, and it will probably go ahead and split it into chapters for you, build out your table of contents, etc. You can drop in your back matter with the click of a button, automatically generate your copyright, and have it laid out for pretty much any print of digital format you could dream of. I got it on sale for Black Friday in 2023.

- **ProWritingAid – Editing**

- My latest acquisition, this is a powerful editing software. For my fiction novels, I'm still hiring editors, but for little zines, free content, and things like that, I'm using ProWritingAid. I already wasn't hiring editors for that type of work anyway, so this acts as a set of eyes that aren't as good as an actual editor, but still better than just my eyes. I got it on sale for Black Friday in 2023.

The Ending: Let's Wrap This Up

I told you this would be short. It's also fairly cheap, though, so you can't complain too much! Well, you can, I guess—just don't expect me to be at all sympathetic. I could have written more, but that would have taken more time away from my main projects than I really needed to spend on a side product. Which, since you've read this book, you now know is a bad thing.

You've come so far.

I am a snarky, silly twit for the most part, but I really feel that if you peel back the bullshit, there is a core pathway here that could take someone someplace. I believe in it enough that I am more or less gambling my life path on it. That may be testament enough, but for most, the proof is in the pudding. Hopefully, when I make it big, I can take the time to write a second version of this book, detailing what I've learned. And here is my promise: If I make it big, I will do so, and there will be a free version of it somewhere.

Just take a damn chance already! I'm not saying to quit your job or anything drastic, but is it really putting you out so much to go buy a few art supplies and knock the dust off your painting skills? Or to write that poem? It's better than you think it is, I can almost promise. Everyone is their own harshest critic. Unless you have some of my professors from college . . . Jesus. They were in a league of their own.

Make your goal. Work towards it. It'll be both harder and easier than you think, but it will certainly be worth it. So, get creative!

And thus, we have now come to the end. If you take nothing else away from this book, let it be this:

Be the change you want to see in the world.

I get it, that's a huge cliche. But sometimes things are cliche for a reason.

Be it in your own life, or the lives of those you care about around you, throw yourself out there and make a difference. I wish you all the success in the world. (Unless you're, I don't know, the next Hitler or something.) And when you're rich and famous and I'm still living in a tiny house in South Alabama, I hope you will remember me fondly. Sip a mimosa in a foreign country in my honor. Or better yet, send me a check! You're rich—you can find me.

Now go buy my shit.

About the author

Born and raised in South Alabama, Bob is an author, podcaster, tabletop game designer, and all around hot mess. His cause of death will most likely result from one of the hitchhikers with he picks up reckless abandon. A study in contrasts, he once skinny-dipped at a wedding and is also an Eagle Scout. He has two useless college degrees, has roadied for bands, and broke his wrist in a wall of death at a Divine Heresy show. He's written for video games, designed board games, and owns a disturbing number of roleplaying games. When he was eight he give a camel a coke in Israel and got flashed in Paris. When he grew up he watched a monkey steal a man's wallet in Costa Rica. He's made passible podcasts, filmed terrible short horror movies, and been the producer on a trio of albums you've never heard of. Thriving on the groans of those he has punned around he spends far too much time nervously laughing. He once dug up a dead cow in a creek thinking it was a human cadaver and had a cousin that's a water witch. In college he gave haunted ghost tours (even though he's pretty sure ghosts aren't real). He's been stalked, gave a Prophet a lift, and been stagger drunk in more states than he would care to admit.

More relevant he wrote this book, some other books, and has been published by a number of other folks with questionable judgement. The fictional things he writes sometimes come weirdly true.

He lives in the middle of Alabama with his amazing LadyWife, the Kiddo, and a number of portly cats.

You can learn more at www.talesbybob.com

Email List!

If you want more Bob content then sign up for my email list! I'll never sell or share my email list, and I promise to never bother you more than once a month (unless it's, like, super-mega-secret important). To sign up, go to my website talesbybob.com.